Architecture in Scotland

Architecture in Scotland

Helmut Petzsch DA (Edin.) FSA Scot.

Plans drawn by
Ian G. Scott DA (Edin.) FSA Scot.

LONGMAN

for Hugo, Linda and Margaret

Longman Group Ltd
London
Associated companies, branches and representatives
throughout the world

© Longman Group 1971

First published 1971
ISBN 0 582 32800 4

Printed in Hong Kong
by Dai Nippon Printing Co., (International) Ltd.

Contents

Map of Scotland

The shaded areas represent regions for which *Inventories*
of the Royal Commission on the Ancient and Historical
Monuments of Scotland have been published.

Illustrations

The following signs are used in the drawings—

 = north point

 = principal entrance

 = photographic viewpoint

F P = fireplace

Doors are left clear and 'window' openings are shown by a double line.
The scale for all the plans is 1:384, except where indicated.
Abbreviations used in the list of buildings to see—
A.M. = Ancient Monument
N.T.S. = National Trust for Scotland

Foreword

I began this book a few years ago, when, as a teacher, I had long felt the need of a well-illustrated introductory guide to the building and architecture of Scotland from prehistory to the present day.

Sites from the early times to the end of the 11th century have been briefly described, thereafter this book has been divided for convenience into sections corresponding to the centuries. Each section is introduced by a short historical account and a note of the architectural character and building activity; a list of buildings to see and books relating to the period is also included. The photographs and plans throughout are all of extant buildings unless otherwise indicated. I have tried to convey an impression of the whole architectural scene in each period, although, in considering the works of the early years especially, allowance must be made for chance survival.

The reader will find it helpful to consult the list of 'buildings to see' in each section and the publications giving information about 'places open to the public' at the beginning of the general reading list. For the sake of completeness I have found it necessary to include some buildings not normally open to the public, though many of these can be conveniently viewed from the outside.

The selection of books on the architecture of particular areas will I hope prove useful to the reader who wishes to know more about a certain locality. The *Lists of Buildings of Architectural or Historic Interest* prepared by the Scottish Development Department are available for inspection at the Department and the offices of the local planning authorities. The National Monuments Record of Scotland have at their offices at 52/54 Melville Street, Edinburgh, an extensive library which can be consulted.

The aim of this guide is to invite the reader to look more inquiringly at the architecture of the country—be it castle, church or house—and to provide him with a selected list of excellent published material from which more information can be obtained.

Since I started this book my work on the subject has been greatly illuminated by the appearance of John G. Dunbar's *The Historic Architecture of Scotland* and the late W. Douglas Simpson's *The Ancient Stones of Scotland,* both of which I recommend to the reader for more extensive reading.

I should like to acknowledge my indebtedness to the staff of the following: the Edinburgh Public Library, the Ministry of Public Building and Works (Edinburgh), the National Building Agency (Scottish Office), the National Library of Scotland, the National Monuments Record of Scotland, the National Museum of Antiquities of Scotland, the National Trust for Scotland, the Saltire Society, the picture library of *The Scotsman,* private and public concerns, and individual architects, all of whom have been most generous in assisting me in my search for illustrative material and information. My sincere thanks are also due to Mr. Colin McWilliam, the late Mr. George Murray, and Mr. Ian G. Scott who also made the drawings, for giving helpful advice and criticism on certain parts of the work; and to the publishers for their interest and encouragement from the outset.

H.P.

Broch, Mousa, Shetland, viewed from the air.

1 Prehistoric

The first peoples to establish settled communities in North Britain were groups of late Stone Age colonists. These were stone-implement-using farming communities who brought with them the specialised knowledge and practical means for mixed farming. They also hunted and fished. Neolithic agriculturalists originated in western Asia and reached the British Isles in increasing numbers over a long period. They came to Scotland by the coastal routes, mainly the west, and display differences of culture in their pottery and burial customs suggestive of different areas of origin. Their areas of colonisation were mainly on the coast, in river valleys and on islands, on good light agricultural land. Though very little is known of their living places, their numerous chambered burial cairns tell us the areas which they had reached. They grew oats and barley and kept domesticated cattle, sheep, goats, pigs and dogs. They made baskets and pottery. Their tools and weapons were made of bone and stone. The stone was fashioned locally and there was trade in specially favoured stone axes from Antrim and the Lake District.

About the second millenium B.C. a new group of colonists began to arrive from the Continent, initially settling along the east coast of Britain. In Scotland the main evidence for their occupation has been discovered in the southern half of the country, the eastern Lowlands and on the islands of Orkney and Shetland. These were also agriculturalists who depended mainly on stone and bone for their tools and weapons, but were the first people to use bronze for weapons and ornaments. They differed from the Neolithic colonists in the custom of burying their dead in individual graves. Tools, weapons and pieces of jewellery were placed in the graves, and there is evidence in Scotland and elsewhere of trading all over Europe. This period is known as the Bronze Age.

It was from about the 2nd century B.C. that the first iron-using communities settled in Scotland. They originated in central Europe and by about 250 B.C. had spread over a great part of the continent and had reached the British Isles. They shared a common language, social organisation, religious traditions, and a style of art commonly labelled Celtic. They bred sheep for their wool, herded cattle, reared horses and grew corn. Weaving implements, as well as domestic utensils, weapons and articles of personal adornment (such as brooches and necklaces), have been found. As settlement sites of various kinds abound we know more about the domestic life of the peoples of the Iron Age than about their predecessors. Roman manuscripts, sculpture and the Irish annals have been other important sources which have contributed to our knowledge of their social habits.

Building activity

Neolithic folk built large chambered tombs for collective burials; some of these are on a magnificent scale and display great skill and organisation in their construction. Of over 350 which have been discovered in Scotland, mainly in the west and north of Scotland and Outer Isles, one of the finest is at Maeshowe in Orkney. Homesteads, on the other hand, are very rare. Post-holes of timber-framed houses with hearths have been discovered. The most notable Neolithic settlement site is at Skara Brae in Orkney; here a cluster of stone-built one-roomed houses connected by passages, with stone furniture, hearths and drains are preserved. In Shetland there are the remains of individual stone-built houses among the pastures, which are surrounded by stone boundary walls. The houses are oval in plan with very thick walls out of which are constructed alcoves facing a central hearth.

Open circular sanctuaries were built in Neolithic times for ceremonial purposes. These were constructed with upright monoliths with and without encircling banks and ditches.

Bronze Age peoples continued the tradition of building stone circles for ceremonial purposes and to enclose burial sites. Their houses were usually circular or oval up to about 12 metres in diameter. Remains show circles of earth and stones with post-holes, a central hearth and sometimes signs of a paved floor. The entrance usually faced south. At Jarlshof in Shetland there is a group of stone-built houses and boundary walls. These houses are roughly oval in plan constructed of thick dry-stone walls and internally divided, with alcoves resembling the chambered tombs and houses of Neolithic times.

Archaeological investigations of the Iron Age have revealed more dwelling sites and fortifications than sacred sites. Celtic tribes in North Britain built round houses of timber, hill fortifications of various types, lake dwellings known as crannogs, underground passages or earth houses called souterrains, and brochs and wheel houses. Their houses were almost always circular in Britain, built of wooden uprights dug into the ground, and could be anything from 6 to 20 metres in diameter. Single houses and groups of such houses forming settlements were generally surrounded by a wooden palisade and bank for security against wild animals, if for no other reason. Crannogs were circular houses built on artificial islands in lakes or bogs, connected to dry land by a wooden gangway. Souterrains are underground galleries, walled and roofed with stone, usually found associated with less permanent buildings above ground. Forts, always occupying defensive sites, were built entirely of stone, or of stone and earth timber-laced with adjacent timber galleries. ('Vitrified' forts, so called, are those in which the wooden parts have been burnt, thus vitrifying or melting the stone.) The latter have been discovered mainly south of the Great Glen; to the north of this line stone fortifications and brochs are more common.

Sites to see
Chambered cairns
Maeshowe, Orkney (A.M.); **Midhowe**, Rousay, Orkney (A.M.); **Unstan Chambered Cairn**, Orkney (A.M.); **Wideford Hill Chambered Cairn**, Orkney (A.M.); **Blackhammer Chambered Cairn**, Rousay, Orkney (A.M.); **Clava Cairns**, Inverness-shire (A.M.); **Grey Cairns**, Camster, Caithness (A.M.); **Nether Largie South Cairn**, Argyll (A.M.).

Neolithic and Bronze Age villages
Skara Brae, Orkney (A.M.); **Jarlshof**, Shetland (A.M.).

Standing stones
Ring of Brogar Stone Circle, Orkney (A.M.); **Ring of Stenness Stone Circle**, Orkney (A.M.); **Loanhead Stone Circle**, Aberdeenshire (A.M.); **Callanish Standing Stones**, Isle of Lewis (A.M.); **Cairnpapple Hill**, West Lothian (A.M.).

Iron Age settlements
White Hill, Peeblesshire; **Hayhope Knowe**, Roxburghshire; **Castlelaw Fort**, Midlothian (A.M.).

Large hill forts or towns
Dunadd Fort, near Kilmichael Glassary, Argyll (A.M.); **Traprain Law**, East Lothian; **Eildon Hill North**, Roxburghshire.

Souterrains
Castlelaw Fort, Midlothian (A.M.); **Rennibister**, Orkney (A.M.); **Ardestie and Carlungie**, Angus (A.M.); **Culsh**, Tarland, Aberdeenshire (A.M.).

Brochs and their forerunners
Mousa, Shetland (A.M.); **Jarlshof**, Shetland (A.M.); **Clickhimin**, Lerwick, Shetland (A.M.); **Gurness**, Aiker Ness, Orkney (A.M.); **Midhowe**, Rousay, Orkney (A.M.); **Dun Carloway**, Lewis, Ross and Cromarty (A.M.); **Dun Beag**, Skye, Inverness-shire; **Dun Telve** and **Dun Troddan**, Glen Elg, Inverness-shire (A.M.).

'Vitrified' forts
Dun Troon, Argyll; **Rahoy**, Argyll; **Finavon**, Angus; **Urquhart Castle**, Inverness-shire (A.M.).

Further reading
CHILDE, V. GORDON and SIMPSON, W. DOUGLAS *Illustrated Guide to Ancient Monuments (Vol. VI Scotland)* Edinburgh, H.M.S.O. 1967
FEACHEM, RICHARD *A Guide to Prehistoric Scotland* London, Batsford 1963
PIGGOTT, STUART *Scotland before History* Edinburgh, Nelson 1958
RIVET, A. L. F. (Editor) *The Iron Age in Northern Britain* Edinburgh, University Press 1966
SCOTT, JACK G. *Regional Archaeologies—South West Scotland* London, Heineman 1966

The earliest builders

Chambered cairns

Megalithic chambered tombs are divided into a number of different types depending upon their internal arrangement. They may ultimately have been derived from a common plan originating in the Eastern Mediterranean.

Midhowe and Maeshowe in Orkney represent two of these. Midhowe is a 'stalled cairn', so called because of the division of the chamber into a number of stalls or recesses to receive the inhumed remains, while at Maeshowe mural cells serve this purpose.

Common to these was the method of building with dry-stone, with walls corbelled inwards to form the roof and the low narrow entrance passage, which was effectively sealed against intruders. The entire structure was covered with earth.

Maeshowe is the most outstanding monument of its class in Britain. The interior is exceptional for the fine masonry work to which the local flagstone lends itself. The illustrations clearly show the method of corbelling the walls inwards to form the roof, and the use of monoliths to form the corners and entrance passage.

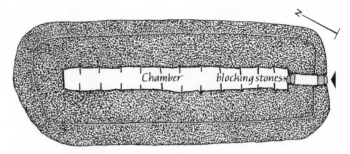

Midhowe (plan).

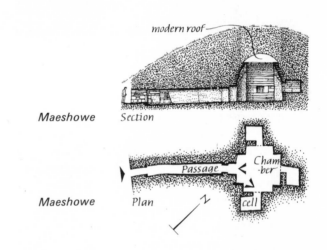

Maeshowe   Section

Maeshowe   Plan

Maeshowe, two interior views.

The Callanish standing stones on the Island of Lewis.

Standing stones

Numerous stone circles built of roughly hewn mono-liths can be seen widely over the country. These impressive monuments of the late Stone Age and Bronze Age indicate sacred sites such as sanctuaries or temples. They were erected on carefully chosen sites and were sometimes enclosed with a ditch and bank.

Prehistoric dwellings

Prehistoric houses in Britain were commonly circular. The preference for this form may have been due to the climatic conditions of the country. Subrectangular forms are known but these are comparatively rare.

Neolithic 'village', Skara Brae, Orkney.

Neolithic house, Shetland (plan).

Post-holes with reconstruction of (?) late Bronze Age or early Iron Age house, West Plean, Stirlingshire.

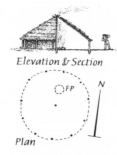

Elevation & Section

Plan

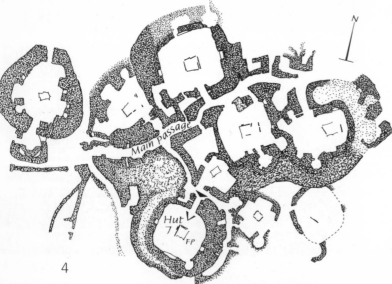

Late Iron Age wheel-house, Jarlshof, Shetland (plan).

4

The discovery of the dwellings at Skara Brae in 1850, after a severe storm had removed their top covering, revealed a site of exceptional antiquarian interest, adding to the knowledge of the domestic life of Stone Age peoples in the northern hemisphere. The walls were constructed of dry-stone and corbelled inwards towards the top. The smoke-hole may have been restricted by skins or turfs resting on a wooden framework. There are no windows. Before excavation these dwellings remained hidden beneath midden refuse and drifting sand. As well as implements of stone and bone, items of personal adornment and pottery were discovered. The main collection has been assembled in the Museum of Antiquities in Edinburgh.

The interior of hut 7, Skara Brae, Orkney. A Neolithic dwelling showing a central hearth, with stone beds and a stone 'dresser' against the walls.

Broch, Mousa, Shetland, viewed from the south-west.

Brochs

The broch, which is unique to Scotland, was developed from the Iron Age stone fortifications introduced by colonising Celts during the 4th to 2nd centuries B.C.

Their sites indicate that good farming land rather than a place of strength was preferred. They are to be found in great numbers either singly or in close proximity to one another, particularly in Caithness, Orkney and Shetland, with a scattering along the west coast and in a few other isolated places. They seem to have been occupied for a fairly short period during the early occupation of Britain by the Romans.

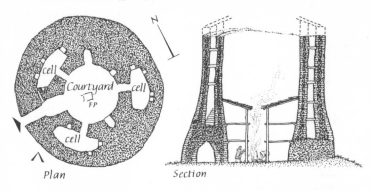

Broch, Mousa (plan).

Plan

Section

A generalised section showing the suggested interior arrangement of a broch.

The broch consisted of a tall circular tower, constructed of dry-stone. The outside walls taper upwards and inwards in a gradual convex-concave outline. In an otherwise featureless wall a small heavily defended entrance passage led to a central courtyard area. The lower walls, of immense thickness, usually contain one or more mural chambers. The upper part is a double wall construction divided horizontally at regular intervals by narrow galleries which run round the cavity. In some a mural stair ascends within the cavity to the wall top. The roof may have been no more than a protection for the wall head. Rising from the courtyard were posts, possibly supporting roofed wooden galleries of two floors, which would have provided accommodation for the inhabitants.

Remains of a broch with a late Iron Age settlement, Jarlshof, Shetland (reconstruction view by Alan Sorrell).

2   The Roman Period c. A.D. 83–343

The Roman occupation of Britain affected Scotland directly though insignificantly. The occupations of Scotland were shortlived, covering only the land south of the Forth and Clyde. There was a penetration as far as Aberdeenshire and a series of permanent strong points were built in southern Perthshire, but before the end of the first century these were evacuated.

Between A.D. 122 and 128, the first formal division between North and South Britain was created when Hadrian's Wall was built. A new advance into Scotland in the period A.D. 139 to 142, resulted in the building of the Antonine Wall across the Forth-Clyde isthmus, of which some of the earthworks can be seen.

Roman building activity in Scotland consisted of the standard pattern of military works as found elsewhere in the Empire—they consisted of forts, marching camps, signal stations and a system of well-built roads with bridges and fords. No Roman villa, town or industrial settlement has been found in Scotland, and only stretches of the earthworks of the Antonine Wall, some forts and roads are now visible.

The domestic building of the native population continued in the tradition of circular huts of rough stone and wood. There is no evidence of dressed stone technique, such as the Romans had used, being used again until about the 10th century.

Sites to see
Legionary fortress
Inchtuthill, Perthshire.

Forts
Ardoch, Perthshire; **Fendoch,** Perthshire; **Birrens,** Dumfriesshire; **Lyne,** Peeblesshire; **Newstead,** Roxburghshire.

Naval bases
Carpow, Perthshire; **Cramond,** Edinburgh.

Antonine Wall
Rough Castle, Stirlingshire (A.M.); **Castle Cary,** Stirlingshire (A.M.).

Further reading
CHILDE, V. GORDON and SIMPSON, W. DOUGLAS *Illustrated Guide to Ancient Monuments* (Vol. VI *Scotland*) Edinburgh, H.M.S.O. 1967

DICKINSON, WILLIAM CROFT *Scotland from earliest times to 1603* Edinburgh, Nelson 1961

RICHMOND, I. A. *Roman Britain* London, Penguin Books 1955

SIMPSON, W. DOUGLAS *The Ancient Stones of Scotland* London, Robert Hale 1965

An aerial view showing the site of the Roman fort at Ardoch, Perthshire. (The earthwork in the centre of the fort is not Roman.) This is the best preserved earthwork of a Roman fort in Scotland. The numerous outer ditches and ramparts are features that occur in several forts in North Britain, and indicate special defensive precautions.

Forts

The usual plan of a permanent fort was rectangular in outline with rounded corners. There was an entrance on each side corresponding with the main roads which ran across the fort at right angles to one another. Buildings were arranged in a regular fashion about this framework with the principal buildings in a central position and the barracks on either side. The size of the fort depended upon the number of men required to garrison it.

3 Fifth to Eleventh Centuries

Four recognisable groups of peoples—Picts, Scots, Britons and Angles—lived in the north of Britain from the 5th century on, and it was not until 1034 that they were united under one king, Duncan. It was to be several centuries yet, however, before all Scotland came under an effective central government.

The earliest Christian foundation in Scotland was St. Ninian's at Whithorn c. 400. But of greater significance and wider influence was St. Columba's Irish Celtic foundation on the island of Iona in 563.

Celtic Christianity from Ireland played an important part in achieving the unification of the country, and although its power waned after the Synod of Whitby (664), when the usages of the Church of Rome were preferred, it bequeathed a literary and artistic heritage of great interest.

From early in the 9th century, peaceful settlements were being made by Norse farmers and fishermen in Orkney, Shetland and in the north and west. These were quite distinct from the preceding Viking raids, which involved the pillaging and destruction of many Christian monasteries.

The marriage of Malcolm III (Canmore) to the Saxon Princess Margaret in 1069 was important in introducing to Scotland the idea of a feudal structure of society, involving certain privileges in return for service and the establishment of knightly castles. There are few records extant from this time which tell us about the social life of the country.

The economy of the country was based chiefly on agriculture. People worked the land and paid tribute to the king or local chief, or to the church, in service or in kind. There was no coinage. Though roads were merely tracks we may presume that the relics of the Roman road system could still be traced. Transport was confined to the pack-horse and boat.

Building activity

With few identifiable exceptions, buildings from the 5th to the 11th centuries are difficult to date and are mostly to be found in remote places. These are widely distributed and provide us with much information about local history. The spread of Christianity and the Norse immigration brought in new building types, but prehistoric and post-Roman Iron Age types continued to be built.

Amongst the early Christian Celtic communities at least two types of buildings seem to have been in use; a small rectangular single-chamber building and a circular 'bee-hive' structure. From about the 10th century Irish and Continental influences are visible. The early Christian monuments and Pictish symbol stones, in contrast to the primitive buildings, serve to illustrate the high standard of artistic achievement during this period.

From early in the 9th century Norse immigrant farming communities settled in the Northern Isles and introduced the 'long-house', from which the Shetland farmhouse seems to be directly descended.

Sites to see

Early Christian sites

Chapel Finian, Wigtownshire (A.M.); **Kirkmadrine,** Wigtownshire (A.M.); **Whithorn Priory,** Wigtownshire (A.M.); **Eileach-an-Naoimh,** Garvelloch Isles, Argyll (A.M.); **St. Cormac's Chapel,** Eilean Mor, Knapdale, Argyll (A.M.); **Iona,** Argyll; **Dunfermline Abbey,** Fife (11th c.) (site of an early church) (A.M.); **Restenneth Priory,** Angus (tower) (A.M.); **Brechin,** Angus (round tower) (A.M.); **Abernethy,** Perthshire (round tower) (A.M.).

Orkney: St. Peter's Church, Birsay (11th and 12th c.) (A.M.); **St. Magnus' Church,** Egilsay (early 12th c.) (A.M.); **St. Tredwell's Chapel,** Papa Westray; **Brough of Deerness; Brough of Birsay.**

Norse settlement sites

Jarlshof, Shetland (A.M.); **Brough of Birsay,** Orkney (A.M.); **Westness,** Rousay, Orkney.

Further reading

CHILDE, V. GORDON and SIMPSON, W. DOUGLAS *Illustrated Guide to Ancient Monuments* (Vol. VI *Scotland*) Edinburgh, H.M.S.O. 1967

CRUDEN, STEWART *Scottish Abbeys* Edinburgh, H.M.S.O. 1960

CRUDEN, STEWART *The Early Christian and Pictish Monuments of Scotland* Edinburgh, H.M.S.O. 1964

DUNBAR, JOHN G. *The Historic Architecture of Scotland* London, Batsford 1966

SINCLAIR, COLIN *The Thatched Houses of the old Highlands* Edinburgh, Oliver & Boyd 1953

SIMPSON, W. DOUGLAS *The Ancient Stones of Scotland* London, Robert Hale 1965

The Early Christian period

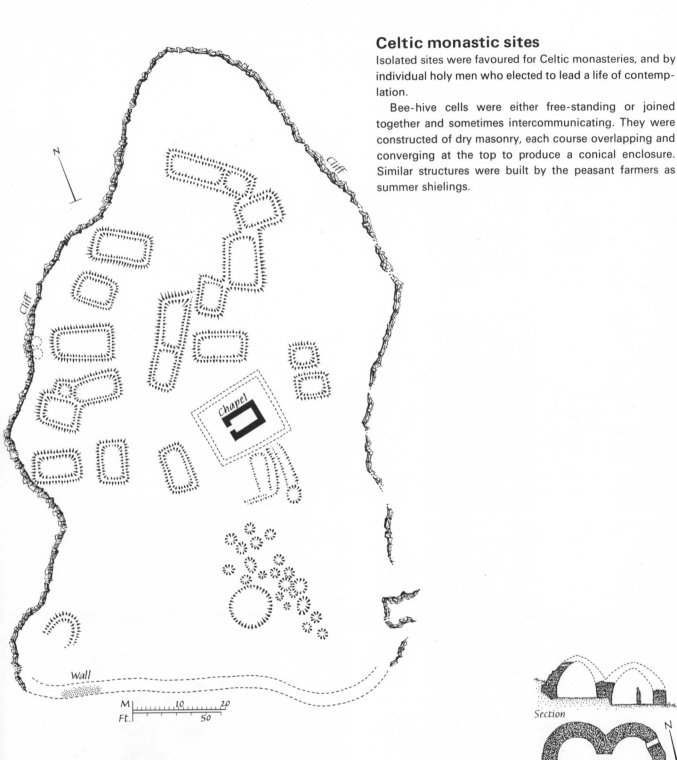

Celtic monastic sites

Isolated sites were favoured for Celtic monasteries, and by individual holy men who elected to lead a life of contemplation.

Bee-hive cells were either free-standing or joined together and sometimes intercommunicating. They were constructed of dry masonry, each course overlapping and converging at the top to produce a conical enclosure. Similar structures were built by the peasant farmers as summer shielings.

The Brough of Deerness, Orkney (plan). A Celtic monastic site showing the random arrangement of rectangular buildings. The settlement is situated on a promontory and enclosed at the southern end by a wall. The chapel is built of flagstones set in clay and pointed with lime mortar.

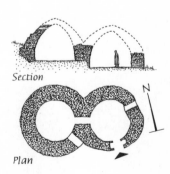

Bee-hive cells at Eileach-an-Naoimh, Argyll

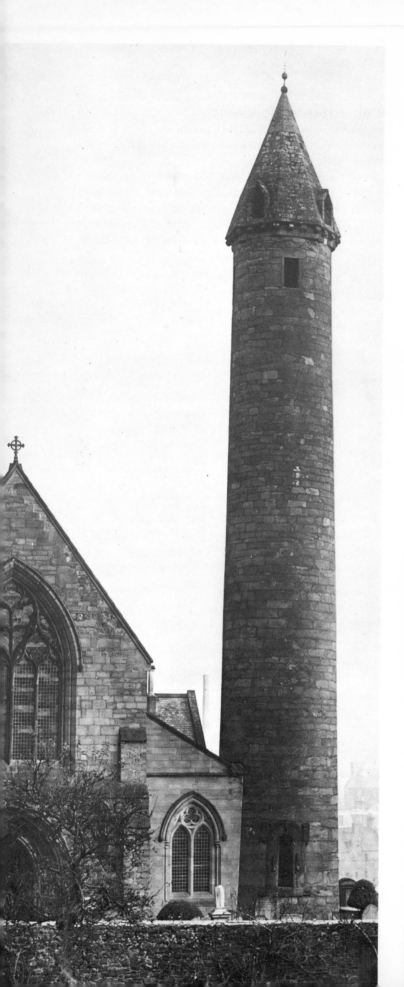

There are two remaining round towers in Scotland of the Irish type. They are evidence of the spread of the Irish Celtic Church into Pictland from the 9th century and indicate the site of a monastic community. They were used as a place of refuge, hence the elevated entrance, and also served as a belfry.

Round tower, Brechin, Angus, c. 1000. The conical roof is a 14th century addition, and may correspond to the original. The narrow round-headed doorway with its inclined jambs has an arched head cut from a single piece of stone. The carved figures and decoration are in the style of the Irish Celtic Church.

The Norse settlement at Jarlshof, Shetland, as it might have looked in the 12th century (reconstruction by Alan Sorrell based on archaeological evidence).

Norse settlements

Settlements such as Jarlshof were built by immigrant farmers from West Norway from early in the 9th century to the 13th century in Shetland and Orkney. Many of the building traditions of these long-houses survive in the later Shetland farmhouses.

The walls were built of stone and infilled with turf. They were roofed with timber and thatch made secure with straw or heather ropes weighted with stones. A hole in the roof allowed the smoke from the central fireplace to filter out. Windows were made in the lower part of the roof. The inhabitants lived at one end and the animals at the other, or in a separate byre.

Churches

An example of an 11th century Norse cathedral is St. Peter's at Birsay. This church consisted of a rectangular nave with a small, almost square quire and a semicircular apse. The quire opened directly out of the nave and is characteristic of other early Orcadian churches built when the Northern Isles were under Norse rule and under the influence of the Irish Romanesque Church.

Under the floor of the Norman nave in Dunfermline Abbey are the foundations of two different but connected buildings. One consists of an oblong nave with a square western tower and, to the east of this, slightly out of

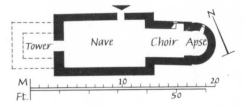

The Norse cathedral. St. Peter's Church, Birsay, Orkney (plan 11th century).

Dunfermline Abbey, Fife (plan of the 10th–11th century church).

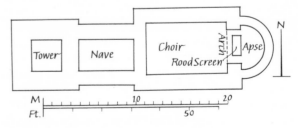

alignment, is a quire with a semi-circular apse, thought to have been erected by Queen Margaret in the 11th century. The plan of this early church is marked on the floor of the existing nave. The 11th century addition marks the introduction of the Norman style of architecture to Scotland. Characteristic of the Norman church is the chancel arch.

Black house, Arnol, Lewis, Ross and Cromarty (exterior).

The interior of the same house showing the open timber roof, central fireplace, and box-bed in a wooden partition.

The 'Black house'

The Hebridean 'black house', which the inhabitants shared with their livestock, is one of a number of traditional house types. The black house recalls primitive origins in construction and general lay-out. It was still being built in the 19th century and remains in small numbers in out-lying parts of the country.

In plan it was sub-rectangular with rounded corners. It was constructed with double walls of rough boulders between which was packed earth or peat mould. The walls might be as much as 2 metres thick. A low-pitched thatch roof, secured with straw rope and stones, rested on the inner walls. This allowed the rain to seep down between the wall faces and compact the earth-filling, which would help to keep out the wind. Small openings in the lower part of the roof or a smoke-hole served for ventilation. There were no windows. The hearth was in the middle of the floor. Clusters of interconnected houses were built on the same lines.

14

4 Twelfth Century

Edgar (1097–1107); Alexander I (1107–24); David (1124–53); Malcolm IV (1153–65); William 'The Lion' (1165–1214).

The kingdom of Scotland, under effective control, consisted of the mainland from the Highland Line south to the Tweed-Solway Line, though for a time under David the English counties of Northumberland, Cumberland and Westmorland were included. The Anglo-Norman influence brought in by Margaret was continued by her sons, especially David. He and his immediate successors introduced military feudalism to Scotland by establishing and developing the Anglo-Norman institutions. Under this system the king was ruler of all the land and the administrator of all justice. By granting a 'fief' (a holding of land) to a great lord who became his 'tenant', the king delegated part of his royal authority. The lord was to maintain law and order there for the king and help him whenever called upon, in return for the enjoyment of the holding and the king's protection. The unit of society became a unit of land, and as David granted most of his fiefs to Norman followers, a French-speaking aristocracy was established which brought lowland Scotland under a well-organised system of government. To enable him to maintain control over his land, each lord was required to build a castle, the Norman motte-and-bailey.

As well as granting land and power to feudal lords, the king built his own castles here and there throughout the kingdom. Each had its royal officer or sheriff with judicial, military, financial and administrative control over a wide area containing several fiefs. Many of these sheriffdoms became the modern shires, e.g., Roxburgh, Stirling. King's burghs were erected beside the castles as their supply centres, and this marks the change from a purely agricultural economy to one of organised trade. The castles and their burghs are to be found on the main lines of communication on the land and by the sea. Other burghs were erected by the church and the lords. A mercantile law governed the burghs, differing from the feudal law, but uniform throughout the kingdom and abroad. The king drew revenue from burgh taxation, and the first Scottish coinage was introduced in David's reign.

The church was reformed to bring it into line with Western Christendom, and was used to support the reorganisation of the state. David founded new religious houses, mostly Cistercian monasteries and Augustinian priories, representative of the two main streams of 12th century monasticism. He restored old episcopal seats and founded new ones, filling most of the important offices with Anglo-Norman clergy. Feudal lords erected churches near their castles to serve themselves and the local community, and at first a system of independent parishes grew up within the diocese. But soon the tithes of the churches were assigned to the abbeys and priories, making them extremely wealthy. Bishops, abbots and priors were important members of the king's council and were sent on embassies abroad.

Building activity
There was a great deal of building—castles, religious houses and burghs, all zealously encouraged by the Canmore dynasty to further the Anglo-Norman control of the kingdom.

Architectural character
Castles, halls and more humble dwellings were built of the materials readily available, unhewn stones, timber, earth and turfs. Nothing of these survives, save one notable example, Castle Sween, Knapdale, in Argyll. The great religious houses, however, were built of stone, in the Romanesque style then prevalent in Western Europe. Master masons were brought in from England and France. The style is recognised by its simple massive forms. The walls were of great thickness, built of dressed stone and filled with rubble. Windows were small and widely spaced. Arches over doors, windows and arcades were semi-circular. Narrow spaces were sometimes vaulted in stone, but for roofing wood was more commonly used. Sculptured decoration was simple but vigorous.

Buildings and sites to see
Early stone castles, built under Norse rule
Castle Sween, Knapdale, Argyll (A.M.); **Cobbie Row's Castle,** Isle of Wyre, Orkney (A.M.).

Motte-and-bailey castles
The Bass, Inverurie, Aberdeenshire; **Huntly Castle,** Aberdeenshire (A.M.); **Duffus Castle,** Morayshire (A.M.); **Urquhart Castle,** Inverness-shire (A.M.); **Mote of Urr,** Kirkcudbrightshire; **Carnwath Motte,** Lanarkshire; **Hawick Motte,** Roxburghshire.

Shell keeps
Doune of Invernochty, Aberdeenshire; **Peel of**

Lumphanan, Aberdeenshire (A.M.); **Rothesay Castle,** Bute (A.M.).

Cathedrals
St. Andrews Cathedral, Fife (A.M.); **St. Magnus Cathedral,** Kirkwall, Orkney; **Dunblane Cathedral,** Perthshire (A.M.).

Monasteries
Dunfermline Abbey, Fife (A.M.); **Arbroath Abbey,** Angus (A.M.); **Dryburgh Abbey,** Berwickshire (A.M.); **Dundrennan Abbey,** Kirkcudbrightshire (A.M.); **Holyrood Abbey,** Edinburgh (A.M.); **Kelso Abbey,** Roxburghshire (A.M.); **Jedburgh Abbey,** Roxburghshire (A.M.).

Churches
St. Regulus Church, St. Andrews, Fife (A.M.); **Dalmeny,** West Lothian; **Leuchars,** Fife; **Tynninghame,** East Lothian; **Dunning,** Perthshire; **Linton,** Roxburghshire; **Muthill,** Perthshire; **Birnie,** Morayshire; **Stobo,** Peeblesshire; **St. Margaret's Chapel,** Edinburgh Castle (A.M.); **Duddingston,** Edinburgh; **Kirkliston,** Uphall, West Lothian.

Further reading

CHILDE, V. GORDON and SIMPSON, W. DOUGLAS *Illustrated Guide to Ancient Monuments* (Vol. VI *Scotland*) Edinburgh, H.M.S.O. 1967
CRUDEN, STEWART *Scottish Abbeys* Edinburgh, H.M.S.O. 1960
CRUDEN, STEWART *The Scottish Castle* Edinburgh, Nelson 1963
DUNBAR, JOHN G. *The Historic Architecture of Scotland* London, Batsford 1966
MACKENZIE, W MACKAY *The Mediaeval Castle in Scotland* London, Methuen 1927
RICHARDSON, JAMES S. *The Mediaeval Stonecarver in Scotland* Edinburgh, University Press 1964
SIMPSON, W. DOUGLAS *Scottish Castles* Edinburgh, H.M.S.O. 1964
SIMPSON, W DOUGLAS *The Ancient Stones of Scotland* London, Robert Hale 1965

Norman and Romanesque

The castle at Dinan (from the Bayeux Tapestry).

Motte-and-bailey castles

The motte-and-bailey castle consisted of a motte, or moated artificial mound, on which was built a wooden tower, the keep, surrounded by a stout stockade. Attached to the motte was a bailey or lower court surrounded by a stockaded bank and ditch, and containing the buildings of the lord's household. A movable ramp gave access from the bailey to the motte, which could thus be defended on its own. An adjacent burgh would be similarly enclosed, with 'ports' for entry, a term which has survived in many towns, e.g., Edinburgh, Netherbow Port.

A Norman motte, The Bass, Inverurie, Aberdeenshire. The area of the top of the motte varied considerably in size, as did the area of the bailey.

Duffus Castle, Morayshire. The motte viewed from the bailey separated by the defensive ditch.

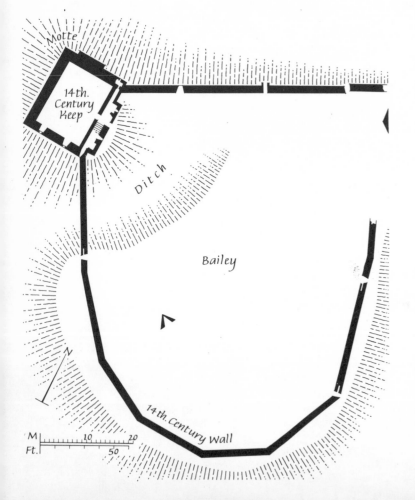

Duffus Castle, Morayshire. A plan showing the motte and bailey. About 1300 a stone tower was built on the motte and a stone wall replaced the timbered earthwork.

Shell keeps

An improvement of the palisaded motte was the 'shell keep'. This consisted of a thick stone wall around the top of the earthwork. When the area so enclosed was large enough, it accommodated buildings of wood and stone for the lord's household, perhaps not unlike the one illustrated on the Bayeux Tapestry (Bosham).

The Peel of Lumphanan is one of two important examples of this type of defensive structure which have been discovered in Scotland. The other is the Doune of Invernochty, also in Aberdeenshire. They date from the end of the 12th and beginning of the 13th century.

Rothesay Castle, Bute, is also a shell keep, but it was extensively added to in later centuries.

The house (from the Bayeux Tapestry) in which Harold feasted at Bosham, showing the hall on the first floor approached by an outside stair over a vaulted basement. This kind of house was common in medieval times and lasted to the 17th century in Scotland.

The Peel of Lumphanan, Aberdeenshire. A shell keep surrounded by a ditch and a rampart.

Early stone castles

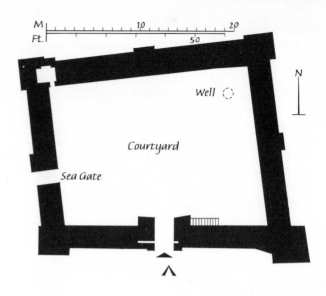

Castle Sween (plan).

The earliest stone castle in Scotland, a keep, Castle Sween, Knapdale, Argyll. The broad flat buttresses and the round arched entrance are characteristic of Norman work. There are no windows, save in the small chamber on the wall-walk. An open stair ascends from the inside of the courtyard of the keep to the wall-walk. High up on the inside of the wall is a chase which carried a timber floor around three-quarters of the courtyard. There is a well in the courtyard. The white line at the entrance is a slot for the draw-bar which secured the door when it was closed.

Dundrennan Abbey, Kirkcudbrightshire, as it might have looked in the mid-13th century (reconstruction by Alan Sorrell).

Dundrennan Abbey, Kirkcudbrightshire (plan).

Monasteries and abbeys

The building of most monasteries in Scotland extended over a long period of time. Consequently different styles can be seen if one looks at the windows and the structural and decorative features.

The plan of Dundrennan Abbey shows a typical monastery. The different monastic foundations were arranged in much the same way; the church orientated east-west, the cloister garth against the south wall of the nave, the sunny side, and the conventual buildings arranged around it. The cloister was usually covered by a wooden lean-to roof. Cistercian foundations were usually built on virgin sites, on good agricultural land. A precinct wall at some distance from the monastery ensured complete seclusion. Examples are to be seen at St. Andrews, Sweetheart and Pluscarden. Entrance was by a defensive gatehouse, to be seen at Arbroath— considered one of the finest in Britain—and St. Andrews.

The monks' range (living quarters) was always placed at the east side of the cloister over the chapter house and sacristy to give access to the church through the south transept. The west side was given over to the lay brothers' range over the cellarage. The space between was occupied by the kitchen, frater (refectory) and common-room (warming-house). The church was divided by a quire (choir) screen, the eastern end reserved for the monks and the western end for the lay brothers. The monks' quire often extended into the nave, because of the short east end.

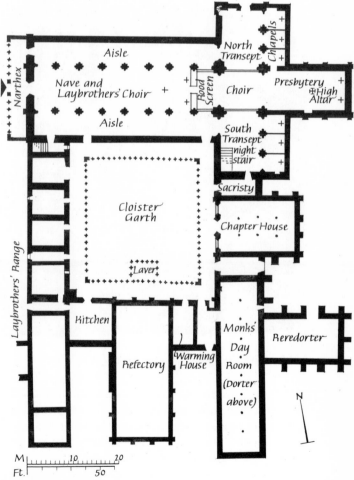

Kelso Abbey, Roxburghshire, exterior of north transept.

The exterior of Norman churches is generally plain with broad flat buttresses projecting at intervals along the walls. Openings are round-arched and recessed in square steps. The circular 'rose' or 'wheel' window built high in the wall made its appearance in this period.

The Norman style is thought to have been introduced into Scotland in the 11th century in the first church built at Dunfermline by Margaret. The foundations of this church (not unlike Dalmeny) are to be seen traced on the floor of the present building which was erected by her son, David I. The characteristics of Norman architecture are here recognised by simple massive forms and semi-circular arches. Norman piers consist of simple cylindrical columns often carved with chevron or spiral lines and topped with bold cushion capitals. The abacus is solid and square-shaped.

Parish churches

These churches were characterised by the same simple massive forms as the great abbeys and cathedrals and, like these, the parish churches could end with either a semi-circular apse or with a square-ended chancel.

Dunfermline Abbey, Fife, the nave.

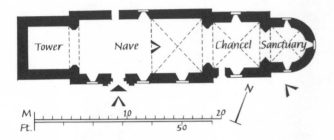

Plan of a typical Norman parish church, based on Dalmeny in West Lothian, which is the most complete. The present tower is a modern reconstruction built on the original foundation.

Dalmeny Church. The roof-line of the building shows clearly the main divisions of nave, chancel and apse.

Dalmeny Church. The interior divisions are punctuated by the decorative arches of the chancel and apse. The ribbed vaulting is exceptionally fine and is limited to the east end. Roofs were commonly of timber and could be painted, as stonework sometimes was.

Dalmeny Church. Main entrance.

Main entrances are generally treated in an ornamental manner, deeply recessed with jambs decorated with a series of round shafts set into square recesses. Arch mouldings are numerous and arranged in receding concentric rings, frequently ornamented with elaborate carving, and enclosing a sculptured tympanum. The only tympanum surviving in Scotland is to be seen at Linton, Roxburghshire.

The entrance to Kilpeck Church, Herefordshire (c. 1145) is included here to illustrate the tympanum.

The church at Leuchars, Fife, where only the chancel and apse remain after the rebuilding of the nave, shows especially fine Norman arcading on the exterior. Tower later.

The tower of a Norman parish church was square, massive and simple. This example at St. Serf's Church, Dunning, is complete, at least to the eaves. It rises to a height of 25 metres to the ridge in three unequal tapering stages. Its unrelieved faces are broken only by horizontal string courses and small openings. The windows in the belfry stage are round-arched and separated by a central shaft.

Decoration

Apart from the Cistercian houses which had an austere simplicity in keeping with the spiritual life of the monks, the religious houses of this period were resplendently ornamented. Walls were richly painted, sculpture was vigorous and bold. Piety, humour, the mundane and the grotesque were depicted side by side.

It is perhaps not difficult to imagine oneself standing inside one of these early churches. The light from the small windows would give a subdued effect to the nave, and one's gaze would be drawn to the chancel with its rich embellishments, and beyond to the altar, glittering with candles.

A fragment of a painted wall decoration from Glasgow Cathedral.

25

5   Thirteenth Century

William I (1165–1214); Alexander II (1214–49); Alexander III (1249–86); disputed succession.

The kingdom in the 13th century corresponded to that of the present day although there was not effective control in the north and west, and Orkney and Shetland belonged to Norway.

It was a century of consolidation; the comparative peace and prosperity were reflected in the large amount of stone building undertaken by the church, the state and the larger barons. The employment of master masons from abroad meant that great building in Scotland came within the traditions of Western Europe.

In the north-east, Celtic earls were accepting Norman feudalism, but in the Western Highlands it remained alien. Most of the important offices of state were held by Anglo-Norman families and French culture predominated at court. Local government continued to be carried out by the sheriffs from the king's castles. The king's officers went round his burghs once or twice a year to ensure that his authority was obeyed. Towards the end of the century we hear of the king's 'parliament', at first chosen by the king from his nobles and the Church to help him as a court of law, later to include representatives elected by the burgesses from the burghs. The burghs' wealth and importance were increasing; they elected their own officers and framed their own laws with regard to trading.

The Church in Scotland expanded, and members of the new orders of friars reached the country in the reign of Alexander II, and soon Franciscans and Dominicans established houses in many burghs.

When Alexander III died the throne was left without a strong heir. The disputed succession plunged the country into untold misery.

Building activity

The 13th century was the age of the stone-built castle. This was a time when new systems of fortifications were being developed in England and France and were introduced to Scotland.

Only the Church, the king and the most powerful barons could afford to build in stone, however, and so most castles and houses continued to be built of wood.

Architectural character

The 13th century saw the introduction of the Gothic style, which had become the main style of architecture in Northern Europe, continuing so until the end of the 15th century, and rather longer in Scotland.

The Gothic Pointed style evolved gradually from the Romanesque style, as builders found a solution to the structural problems involved when arches of different widths were used together to produce the same height. The pointed arch had been used in buildings together with the round arch during the period of transition, e.g. Jedburgh Abbey, but it gradually replaced the round arch entirely. 'First Pointed' is the name given to the earliest developed phase of Gothic.

The general character of Gothic architecture, particularly in churches, was one of height and gracefulness. This was due to the universal use of the pointed arch, the pronounced buttress and the vertical emphasis of the pier. Walls were less massive. Vaulting over narrow areas was generally of the rib and panel kind, though main roofs continued to be built of timber. Sculptured decoration was more refined, with pronounced mouldings and conventionalised forms from nature.

Buildings to see
Simple castles of enclosure
Castle Roy, Inverness-shire; **Tioram Castle**, Inverness-shire; **Mingary Castle**, Ardnamurchan, Argyll; **Skipness Castle**, Kintyre, Argyll; **Loch Doon Castle**, Ayrshire (A.M.); **Kisimul Castle**, Barra, Outer Hebrides.

Castles of enclosure with flanking towers
Lochindorb Castle, Morayshire; **Inverlochy Castle**, Inverness-shire (A.M.); **Kinclaven Castle**, Perthshire; **Balvenie Castle**, Banffshire (A.M.); **Dunstaffnage Castle**, Lorn, Argyll (A.M.); **Rothesay Castle**, Bute (A.M.).

Great castles of enclosure
Kildrummy Castle, Aberdeenshire (A.M.); **Bothwell Castle**, Lanarkshire (A.M.); **Dirleton Castle**, East Lothian (A.M.); **Caerlaverock Castle**, Dumfriesshire (A.M.).

Hall-houses
Rait Castle, Nairnshire (A.M.); **Morton Castle**, Dumfriesshire; **Tulliallan Castle**, Fife; **Hailes Castle**, East Lothian (A.M.); **Yester Castle**, East Lothian; **Skipness Castle**, Kintyre, Argyll.

Religious houses
Holyrood Abbey, Edinburgh (A.M.); **Jedburgh Abbey**,

Roxburghshire (A.M.); **Paisley Abbey,** Renfrewshire; **Dundrennan Abbey,** Kirkcudbrightshire (A.M.); **Dryburgh Abbey,** Berwickshire (A.M.); **Inchcolm Abbey,** Fife (A.M.); **Coldingham Priory,** Berwickshire; **Pluscardine Priory,** Morayshire.

Cathedrals
Glasgow Cathedral (A.M.); **Dunblane Cathedral,** Perthshire; **Elgin Cathedral,** Morayshire (A.M.); **Brechin Cathedral,** Angus.

Parish churches and chapels
Kilmory, Knap, Knapdale, Argyll (A.M.); **Auchindoir,** Aberdeenshire; **Barevan,** Nairnshire; **Killean,** Kintyre, Argyll; **Skipness,** Kintyre, Argyll; **Dunstaffnage,** Lorn, Argyll (A.M.); **Preston,** East Lothian; **Pencaitland,** East Lothian; **Airth,** Stirlingshire; **St. Kentigern's,** Lanarkshire; **Cowie,** Kincardineshire; **Kincardine O'Neil Kirk,** Kincardineshire; **Abdie Church,** Fife.

Further reading
CHILDE, V. GORDON and SIMPSON, W. DOUGLAS *Illustrated Guide to Ancient Monuments* (Vol. VI Scotland) Edinburgh, H.M.S.O. 1967
CRUDEN, STEWART *Scottish Abbeys* Edinburgh, H.M.S.O. 1960
CRUDEN, STEWART *The Scottish Castle* Edinburgh, Nelson 1963
DUNBAR, JOHN G. *The Historic Architecture of Scotland* London, Batsford 1966
MACKENZIE, W. MACKAY *The Mediaeval Castle in Scotland* London, Methuen 1927
RICHARDSON, JAMES S. *The Mediaeval Stonecarver in Scotland* Edinburgh, University Press 1964
SIMPSON, W. DOUGLAS *Scottish Castles* Edinburgh, H.M.S.O. 1964
SIMPSON, W. DOUGLAS *The Ancient Stones of Scotland* London, Robert Hale 1965

Tioram Castle, Loch Moidart, Inverness-shire.

Early or First Pointed Gothic period

The earliest existing stone castles in Scotland consist of a single high wall of enclosure, called a curtain wall, enclosing a courtyard area. The substantial curtain walls were built of stone and lime with a rubble core.

Castles of enclosure

On the western seaboard there are a number of castles of enclosure which rise to a considerable height and finish in a crenellated wall-walk. A number of these occupy sites of strength on irregular rocky outcrops which have determined their layout. They are easily defended because of their site and most depended on the sea for communications. They have one or two small entrances, generally one to landward and one to the sea, a few very small windows and strategically placed firing slits. Internally, buildings of wood or stone were erected against the wall of enclosure which in some cases had mural chambers. Mingary Castle is one of these.

When simple castles of enclosure were not built on a natural place of strength, their plan was more often quadrangular and they were provided with outer defences such as ditches or a moat and ramparts.

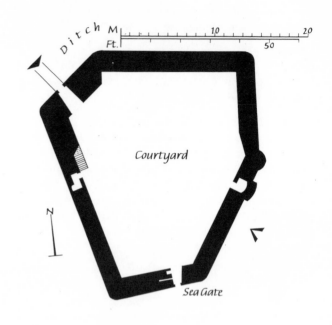

Mingary Castle, Argyll (plan).

Mingary Castle, Ardnamurchan, Argyll, viewed from the east.

New developments in methods of warfare in the 13th century, including such devices as assault towers, mechanised catapults, and armoured battering-rams, were soon followed by improvements in the design of castles.

Round corner towers rising from the ground to the wall head were incorporated in the curtain-wall castle, giving the defenders a better view of the foot of the wall. Such castles were called 'enceinte'. Later one of these towers was built large enough to form a secure refuge in time of siege when the main enclosure had been broached. This came to be called the 'keep' tower or 'donjon' and usually occupied a position farthest from the entrance. The donjon had much the same relationship to the area enclosed by the curtain wall as the motte had to the bailey. The plan of Inverlochy Castle illustrates these points well.

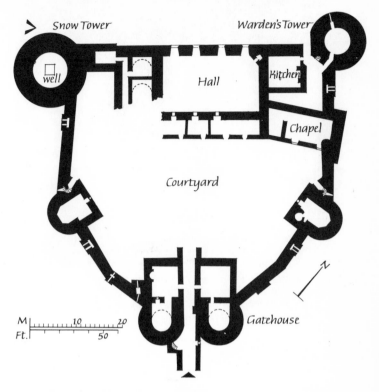

Kildrummy Castle, Aberdeenshire (plan).

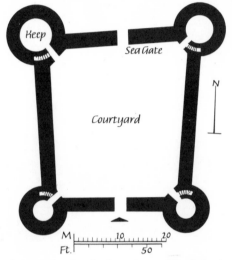

Inverlochy Castle, Inverness-shire (plan).

Towards the end of the century a further improvement in defence was introduced when the gate-house, the most vulnerable part of the castle, was strengthened with flanking towers and guard rooms (Bothwell and Kildrummy). This is typical of the great castles of enclosure associated with the Plantagenet era.

The base of the 'Snow Tower', the donjon of Kildrummy Castle. It illustrates the spreading base, called a plinth, which gave greater protection at the foot of the wall, and the fine masonry, which was usual in the greater castles of this time. The long slit of the distant Warden's Tower gave flanking cover between the towers; in this way the outside walls were defended from a lower level.

The Warden's Tower, Kildrummy Castle, showing the inside of the arrow slit, which is about 2 metres tall, and the deep embrasure sufficiently large to accommodate two men operating cross bows.

From about the middle of the century further developments of the great curtain-wall castles were taking place, when the keep tower was brought forward to the entrance and incorporated in it to form the 'keep gate-house'—Dirleton and Caerlaverock.

Notable features in the well-fortified curtain-wall castles at the turn of the century are illustrated in the reconstruction view of Dirleton Castle. In addition to the crenellated wall-head (a) are overhanging wooden galleries (b), called hoardings, which protected the defenders while allowing them to keep an eye on the foot of the wall. The dry ditch or moat was bridged. A drawbridge protected the entrance (c), which could be closed with a portcullis. At some convenient point in the main wall there was usually a 'postern', a very small easily guarded side entrance (d).

Dirleton Castle, East Lothian (reconstruction by Alan Sorrell, showing what it might have looked like in the 14th century).

Dirleton Castle, 13th century, as it stands to-day, viewed from the south.

Dirleton Castle (plan).

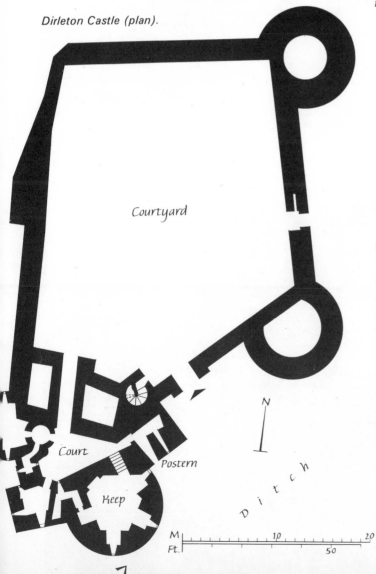

Hall houses

The hall house, or fortified manor house, appears in Scotland in small numbers at the end of the 13th century and beginning of the 14th. This type of building bears a close resemblance to the type more numerous in England, whence it was probably introduced. It consists of an oblong unvaulted hall above a cellar. In the example illustrated a circular tower extended from one corner and this formed the lord's private apartment. At the opposite end of the hall, a screen separated the hall from the service end or 'screens' passage. The entrance was at hall level and was defended with a portcullis and heavy door secured by a drawbar, and was reached by a wooden stair or retractable ladder. The whole was originally surrounded by a walled enclosure with round towers.

Security at the entrance as well as at the perimeter was usual for a baronial residence and continued to be the

31

dominant factor in Scottish building till the early part of the 17th century. It was more vulnerable than the tower-house which features in the 14th century and thereafter. This may have been the reason for the unpopularity of this type of dwelling.

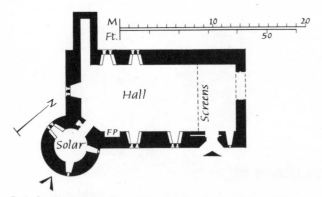

Rait Castle (plan). The absence of a kitchen suggests that this was provided for by a separate building, a fairly common arrangement.

Rait Castle. A window embrasure in the solar built within the thickness of the wall and flanked with stone seats—a domestic feature commonly seen in medieval architecture.

Rait Castle, Nairnshire, viewed from the south. The larger opening is the entrance. The hall would have been roofed with timber. The Gothic pointed arch is typical of windows and doors of the 13th century.

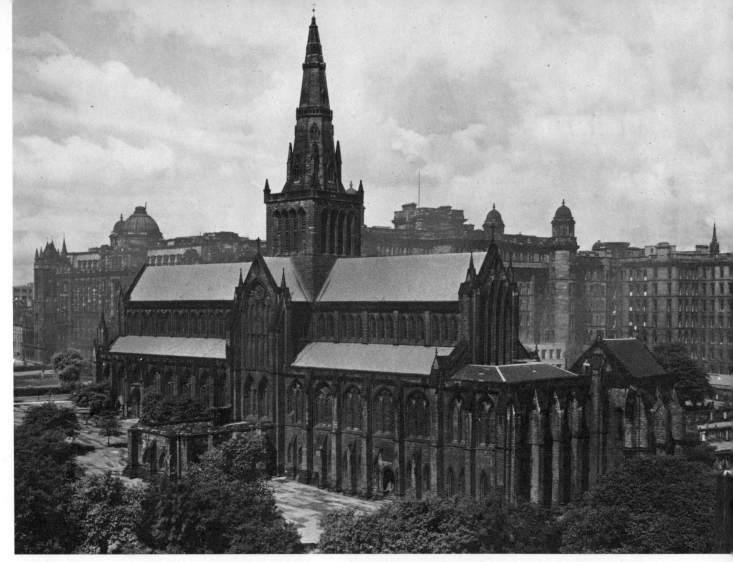

Glasgow Cathedral, which is the only complete medieval cathedral surviving on the mainland, was built chiefly in the 13th and 14th centuries. This exterior view shows the vertical tendency which is so characteristic of Gothic architecture. Originally two attached towers stood at the western end (see plan) but these were removed in the 19th century. Notice particularly the large size of the windows, and the vertical buttresses which projected from between them. These were necessary to strengthen the walls which had to take the weight of the stone vaulting of the aisles. The absence of pronounced buttresses in the clerestory is because of the preference for the wooden roof, which was more common in Scotland and England than in France where the style originated. The tower and spire were built in the 15th century replacing a wooden spire.

Cathedrals

In the reorganised church of the 12th century, the cathedral was the principal church of the diocese.

Glasgow Cathedral (plan). The crossing, which is formed by the transepts, does not project beyond the aisles.

This view of the interior, from the nave into the quire, gives an impression of height and elegance, created by the vertical lines of the clustered piers (a), the ribbed arches (b), the tall narrow windows and the pointed arch. The quire screen (c) (late 15th century), separating the nave from the quire, was a usual feature in all large medieval churches. The quire (eastern half) was built in the mid-13th century and shows the developed First Pointed style; the nave (western half) was built in the latter part of the 13th century and the beginning of the 14th century and shows the later development of the First Pointed, i.e. the early Decorated style of Gothic. To appreciate the difference between Norman and Gothic, compare this view with the interior of Dunfermline Abbey (12th century).

A view of the north-east angle of the quire, showing the quire arcade (a), the triforium (b), and the clerestory (c). Notice particularly the tall lancet windows of the east end, and the diamond shape piers which are so built to support the ribbed arches.

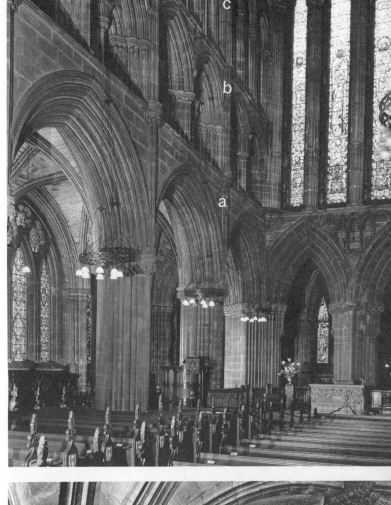

Another notable feature of Glasgow Cathedral is the lower church, which houses the Shrine of St. Mungo. This has remarkably fine rib vaulting which supports the quire. The intricately carved stone (a) at the termination of the ribs is called a boss.

Churches and chapels

Parish churches and chapels built in the 13th century were mostly long and narrow with an entrance in one of the long walls, usually the southern one. A few tall, narrow single-light windows were built in the south and east walls. These were sometimes decorated on the inside with surrounding mouldings, detached shafts and Gothic and Romanesque detail. A timber screen separated the chancel from the nave.

Kilmory Chapel is a typical medieval church of the West Highland type. They consisted of a single chamber (unicameral) with an entrance in the sidewall near the western end. Windows were few and small, with wide splays on the inside and little or no decorative treatment. The roof would have been built of timber covered with thatch.

Because they were built in this simple form over a long period they are difficult to date with accuracy.

Dunstaffnage Chapel, Lorn, Argyll.

Plan based on Dunstaffnage Chapel.

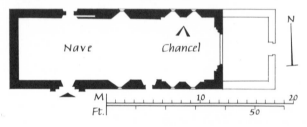

The southern entrance to the fine church of St. Mary at Auchindoir is a good example of the Norman Transitional style.

Chapel, Kilmory, Knapdale, Argyll.

6 Fourteenth Century

Robert I (1306–29); David II (1329–71): Robert II (1371–90); Robert III (1390–1406).

Robert the Bruce achieved independence for Scotland, but at his death trouble broke out again. The lack of a strong leader, the personal ambitions and vacillating allegiances of the important nobles, many of whom, being of Anglo-Norman descent, held lands in England and France as well as in Scotland, dislocated trade and brought great misery to the people. Social, cultural and diplomatic relations with neighbours were disrupted; law and authority were overthrown. To the end of the century the ordinary people had a bitter struggle for existence because of the lack of social organisation, economic conditions, the abuses of the church, famine and the Black Death.

The physical nature of Scotland both helped and hindered its development. The lowlands were fertile, but gave easy access and plunder to marauders from the south; the mountainous regions were almost barren, but favoured defensive guerilla warfare.

The poorness of the Highland soil and the continual warfare amongst the clans themselves made life precarious. These clans were made up of a related group of families who acknowledged the authority of no one but their chieftain. The Anglo-Norman feudal system was never completely integrated as it was in England; opposition from the old Celtic system of society took long to overcome.

The burghs were growing in importance at this time, however, and the overseas trade of the merchants was the principal source of wealth for the nation and revenue for the king. The burgesses became more important in the 'parliament' and we now hear of the 'Three Estates' — Churchmen, Nobles and Burgesses.

Building activity
The Wars of Independence and their aftermath wrought havoc in the country and brought building of every description almost to a standstill. Church building was particularly affected and a great many monasteries and abbeys were destroyed.

Unsettled conditions were responsible for the noble and laird adopting the tower-house as a residence, a modest structure which provided the necessary security.

The building of large castles was discouraged and the few that were built and earlier ones that were altered begin to show a change which was current in Europe.

By the end of the century the medieval conception of a stronghold was obsolete. Its place began to be taken by the castle with out-buildings around a courtyard, including a substantial tower controlling the entrance. Though guns were used in the 14th century, they did not bring about an immediate change in the methods of defence in castles.

The frequent references to the burning of towns and their fairly rapid rebuilding indicates timber buildings. For the ordinary country folk, houses would have been of the simplest kind, built of whatever material came to hand.

Architectural character
When the First Pointed style of Gothic architecture developed a more decorative appearance, it is given the name 'Decorated' or 'Middle Pointed' style. This is most easily seen in the windows of the period which now tend to become broader and use less stone between the lights, the upper part of the window being filled with geometric tracery. In castles, carved Gothic decoration is seen to some extent in windows and fireplaces. Barrel vaults were either pointed or round. The development of the Gothic style in Scotland was arrested by unsettled conditions and it is not until the beginning of the 15th century that we see a change.

Buildings to see
Tower-houses (rectangular plan)
Drum Castle, Aberdeenshire (late 13th and 14th c.); **Carrick Castle**, Argyll; **Threave Castle**, Kirkcudbrightshire (A.M.); **Dundonald Castle**, Ayrshire (A.M.); **Duffus Castle**, Morayshire (A.M.); **Hallforest Tower**, Aberdeenshire; **Crichton Castle**, Midlothian (A.M.); **Torthorwald Castle**, Dumfriesshire; **Lochleven Castle**, Kinross-shire (A.M.); **Aberdour Castle**, Fife (A.M.); **Clackmannan Tower**, Clackmannanshire (A.M.).

Tower-houses ('L' plan)
Craigmillar Castle, Edinburgh (A.M.); **Neidpath Castle**, Peeblesshire, (late 14th c); **Dunnottar Castle**, Kincardineshire.

Great castles of enclosure
Tantallon, East Lothian (14th c. and later) (A.M.); **Doune**, Perthshire (late 14th c.); **Balvenie Castle,** Banffshire (in part 14th c.) (A.M.).

Abbeys, cathedrals and churches

New Abbey or **Sweetheart Abbey,** Kirkcudbright-shire (A.M.); **Elgin Cathedral,** Morayshire (13th c., late 14th c. and later) (A.M.); **St. Giles Church,** Edinburgh (late 14th c.); **St. Monance Church,** Fife (late 14th. c. and 15th c.); **Fortrose Cathedral,** Ross and Cromarty (late 14th c.) (A.M.); **Lincluden College,** Kirkcud-brightshire (late 14th c. and 15th c.) (A.M.); **Glasgow Cathedral** (13th c. and early 14th c.) (A.M.); **Melrose Abbey,** Roxburghshire (late 14th–15th c.) (A.M.).

Further reading

CHILDE, V. GORDON and SIMPSON, W. DOUGLAS *Illustrated Guide to Ancient Monuments* (Vol. VI *Scotland*) Edinburgh, H.M.S.O. 1967

CRUDEN, STEWART *Scottish Abbeys* Edinburgh, H.M.S.O. 1960

CRUDEN, STEWART *The Scottish Castle* Edinburgh, Nelson 1963

DUNBAR, JOHN G. *The Historic Architecture of Scotland* London, Batsford 1966.

MACKENZIE, W. MACKAY *The Mediaeval Castle in Scotland* London, Methuen 1927

RICHARDSON, JAMES S. *The Mediaeval Stonecarver in Scotland* Edinburgh, University Press 1964

SIMPSON, W. DOUGLAS *Scottish Castles* Edinburgh, H.M.S.O. 1964

Middle or Decorated Gothic period

Tower-houses

The tower-house, as its name implies, is a tall vertical building of castle-like appearance, consisting of one room on each floor connected by a mural stair, rising to a low saddle-back roof of slabbed stone which is encircled by a wall walk and crenellated parapet

Its popularity with the lesser barons, the lairds and the smaller landholders reflected the unsettled conditions prevailing in the country. Its essentially simple form lent itself to many interesting variations to suit the demands of comfort and security over a considerable time.

The number of this type of fortified house built in Scotland from the 14th to the 17th century over the entire country was greater than the combined total of all other types of fortified buildings.

In its simplest form it was square or rectangular on plan. The severely plain walls were broken only by small irregularly placed openings for ventilation and light. There were no arrow-slits, as there were in medieval strong-holds. Entrance was gained at ground, first or second floor level by a timber stair or ladder. The entrance was closed with a stout wooden door behind which hung an iron grille or 'yett' (see page 77).

The main room was the hall, generally on the first floor over a vaulted cellar, with sometimes a hatch in the floor for communication. Above the hall rose a tall barrel vault (see page 44) and sometimes a second one to the roof with wooden floors between them. Mural chambers, cupboards and garderobes were built into the thick walls which were constructed of rubble and lime.

The tower-house was surrounded by a low enclosure wall, called a barmkin, within which stood out-buildings and stables, and the kitchen when this was not included in the tower. Often more substantial all-round defence was provided by a ditch or a moat and rampart.

The Castle of Drum in Aberdeenshire is one of these early tower-houses. It was built in the late 13th or early 14th century and is still occupied by the descendants of the family who built it. The plainness of the rubble walls is relieved in their upper storeys by a shallow corbel course above which the crenellated parapet breaks the sky-line. The corners of the parapet rise above the sides and add a note of dignity to the composition of the tower as a whole. This feature was to become more pronounced in the 15th century. The rounded corners are not uncommon in early castles. (The large window and the adjacent buildings are later.)

Castle of Drum, viewed from the north-east.

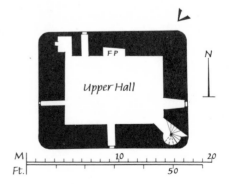

Castle of Drum, Aberdeenshire. Plan of the second floor.

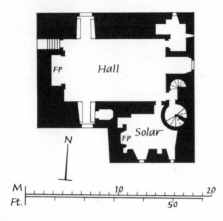

Craigmillar Castle, Edinburgh. Plan of the first floor.

In the second half of the 14th century changes began to be introduced into the tower-house which reflected a desire for greater comfort. The plan of the first floor of Craigmillar Castle, Edinburgh, shows this. Additional mural chambers, cupboards called aumbries and the increased size of the window embrasures with stone seats were fairly typical. The inclusion of a short wing, or 'jamb', protruding from one side provided more accommodation and greater privacy. The addition of the jamb made the plan 'L' shaped, which serves to describe this type.

In the 'L' plan tower-house, the entrance was commonly built on the ground floor in the re-entrant angle. In most other respects the tower-house of the late 14th century did not differ in appearance from the earlier ones.

Castles of enclosure

Representative of their period are Tantallon Castle, East Lothian, and Doune Castle, Perthshire.

Tantallon Castle has a curtain wall with a fully-developed keep gate-house. It was built by a powerful magnate of the realm on an impregnable promontory jutting into the sea.

The massive curtain wall straddles the promontory forming a courtyard which contained the hall and other ranges. At the centre of the wall is the well-defended keep—the Mid Tower which controlled the entrance. A notable feature is the forward position of the tower, which was extended with a barbican by the end of the century, so stressing the importance of this system of defence. At either end of the curtain were massive circular towers connected to the keep by a wall walk.

The landward approach to the castle was defended by ramparts and ditches. A sea gate was built on the north-east cliff forming the only other entrance. The long, narrow firing-slits, the crenellated wall-head and the absence of windows leave one in no doubt about its defensive intentions.

Built at the end of the 14th century, Doune Castle, Perthshire, was not a defensive stronghold like Kildrummy, nor a great keep gate-house like Tantallon, but a fortified baronial residence. It was built for the Regent Albany, Governor of Scotland, and was intended as a courtyard castle, i.e. a castle comprised of ranges of buildings enclosing and facing into an open courtyard, but it was never completed.

Doune Castle represents the transition between the

Tantallon Castle, East Lothian. A bird's-eye view.

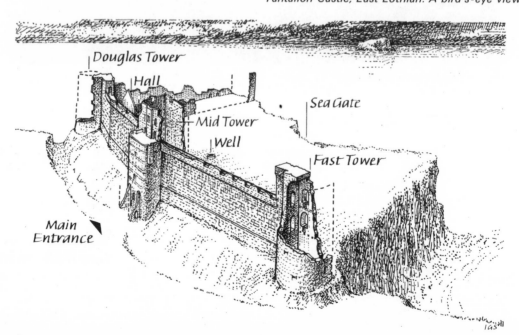

keep gate-house castle and the courtyard castles of the 15th century and later. Like the great keep gate-house castles, it was designed for accommodating a large retinue with a self-contained tower for the lord at the entrance. This gave him the control necessary when the loyalty of the hired soldiers could not be depended upon.

The lord's tower over the entrance is served by a private stair from within the courtyard to the 'screens' passage in the hall. Above the hall were his private chambers. Adjoining the main tower and originally not communicating with it, stands a horizontal block containing the retainers' hall with a central fireplace and an open timber roof. Beneath this hall are storage cellars. The kitchen is in a tower apart served with its own stair, and communicating through a service room with the retainers' hall.

The courtyard is enclosed on the remaining sides with a substantial wall crowned with a wall walk. Open turrets, or bartizans, project upon stepped stone brackets, or corbels, from the wall-head of the castle, but there are no flanking towers and no long firing-slits. Instead we see some large windows looking outward which contradict its martial appearance and indicate rather a splendid baronial residence.

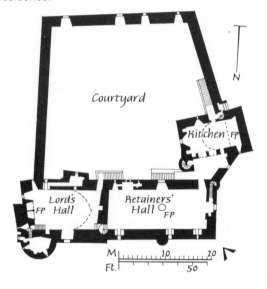

Doune Castle, Perthshire. Plan of the first floor.

Doune Castle. View from the north-west.

New Abbey, or Sweetheart Abbey, Kirkcudbrightshire. The large east window in the presbytery is an example of the development of Gothic window tracery of this period. The narrow lights were constructed with stone shafts called mullions and traceried heads to form geometric patterns and were enclosed in a moulded arch.

42

Melrose Abbey, blind arcading of Late Decorated style in the cloister.

Abbeys and churches

The Second Pointed or Decorated style of Gothic which evolved in the 14th century continued until about the middle of the 15th. This was longer than in England and France, but during this time Scotland was almost entirely cut off from the sources of architectural developments. She had no master masons of great calibre of her own and the continuance in the Gothic tradition was uninspired. Designs were less refined than in the 13th century and show a lack of understanding of the architectural principles of the style. On the whole it is not until the second half of the 15th century that we begin to see better examples of the late Gothic style by native craftsmen.

The eastern part of Melrose Abbey is a seeming exception, but it was not built by Scottish masons. It was twice destroyed in the 14th century, latterly by Richard II of England, who, it is thought, started its rebuilding, using master masons from the school of York.

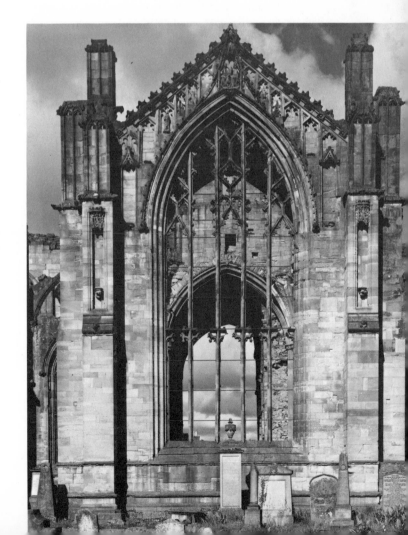

Melrose Abbey, the great east window.

Melrose Abbey, Roxburghshire, viewed from the south-west.

The illustrations of the south transept and the upper half of the great east window show respectively Late Decorated and Early Perpendicular style of Gothic architecture of a very high order. The great east window is thought to be the work of the York school of masons, while the south transept is the work of the French master mason who took over the work in the 15th century when the abbey ceased to be under English control.

The window tracery of the south transept shows how the Late style evolved from the geometric forms of the early 14th century. These are now formed into curvilinear and flamelike forms, sometimes called flamboyant. In the great east window the mullions have been taken to the head of the window and the spaces filled with intricate carved tracery like lacework. Carved decoration was not confined to the windows, as these illustrations show, but covered much of the exterior and interior. The niches (a) on the buttresses contained statues, some of which have survived. Over the south aisle are 'flying' buttresses (b), which support the nave vault (a rare example in Scotland). The buttresses are capped with carved pinnacles (c).

Rib-and-panel stone vaulting. St. Mary's Aisle, Elgin Cathedral, Morayshire.

Solid barrel stone vaulting of pointed section. Crichton Castle, Midlothian.

7 Fifteenth Century

Robert III (1390–1406); James I (1406–37); James II (1437–60); James III (1460–88); James IV (1488–1513).

The history of the 15th century is again the story of the struggle between the king and his too-powerful nobles. James I ruled vigorously and introduced through Parliament important financial and administrative reforms to bring law and order to the country. He also tried to prevent the drain of money to the Church in Rome and to gain some control over the appointment of churchmen, as these men formed an important part of his Parliament and Council.

James II was a strong king, but died early; James III was weak and unpopular. James IV established a firm rule and the country progressed. He brought the Highlands and Islands under his control. The trading ports on the east coast grew and there was an expanding economy with changing standards of living and an interest in the arts. The end of medievalism was in sight with a wave of new thinking sweeping through Europe. Three universities were founded in Scotland in this century and an Education Act was passed laying down that the eldest sons of substantial barons and freeholders were to attend school.

Edinburgh's importance grew and it was accepted as the principal burgh of the kingdom. James IV built the Palace block at the Castle and centralised the courts of law in Edinburgh. The burghs increased in importance in national affairs as the wealth of the merchants increased.

Early artillery was costly and remained, to begin with, the prerogative of the king. It was used for a long time to supplement and not replace traditional implements of warfare. Consequently there was little change in castle design, with one notable exception, Ravenscraig Castle.

Building activity

The king started new building at his castles and palaces. Troubled times were responsible for the continued popularity of the tower-house which made this the most representative building of the 15th century. The limited use of guns had little effect on the design of the castle. Collegiate churches (see page 52) became more common and the burghs' prosperity was reflected in the rebuilding of their churches. The earliest stone bridges date from this time.

Stone was more widely used; though most buildings in burghs were still of wood, no doubt some would have been built of stone.

Architectural character

In castellated architecture more attention was being given to domestic requirements. Larger castles were altered and ranges of buildings were added which often then assumed a courtyard layout. The design of the tower-house developed further to provide better accommodation and the wall-head became more pronounced. The high pointed barrel-vault was more widely used in castles and churches.

Ecclesiastical architecture received a renewed impetus from the establishment of collegiate and new burgh churches. Castellated and domestic architectural forms begin to appear in church building. Piers were either diamond-shaped, polygonal or round. Carved enrichments including heraldry were more common.

The Decorated style of Gothic predominated but there was a revival of Romanesque features.

Buildings to see

Tower-houses (rectangular plan)

Burleigh Castle, Kinross-shire (A.M.); **Cardoness Castle**, Kirkcudbrightshire (A.M.); **Comlongon Castle**, Dumfriesshire; **Newark Castle**, Selkirkshire; **Sauchie Tower**, Clackmannanshire; **Liberton Tower**, Edinburgh; **Huntingtower Castle**, Perthshire (15th–16th c.) (A.M.); **Mearns Tower**, Renfrewshire; **Benholm Castle Tower**, Kincardineshire; **Falside**, East Lothian; **Dean Castle**, Ayrshire.

Tower-houses ('L' plan)

Merchiston Castle, Edinburgh (15th c. and later); **Clackmannan Tower**, Clackmannanshire (A.M.); **Preston Tower**, East Lothian; **Huntly Castle**, Aberdeenshire (A.M.); **Affleck Castle**, Angus (A.M.); **Dundas Castle**, West Lothian.

Tower-houses of unusual plan

Borthwick Castle, Midlothian; **Orchardton Tower**, Kirkcudbrightshire (A.M.); **Hermitage Castle**, Roxburghshire (A.M.).

Tower-houses with later additions built round a courtyard

Crichton Castle, Midlothian (A.M.); **Castle Campbell**, Clackmannanshire (A.M.); **Craigmillar Castle**, Edinburgh (A.M.); **Huntly Castle**, Aberdeenshire (A.M.).

Royal castles and palaces
Edinburgh Castle, the Palace (A.M.); **Linlithgow Palace,** West Lothian (A.M.); **Stirling Castle,** the Great Hall (A.M.); **Falkland Palace,** Fife (N.T.S.); **Ravenscraig Castle,** Kirkcaldy, Fife (A.M.).

Collegiate churches
Lincluden College, Kirkcudbrightshire (A.M.); **Corstorphine Church,** Edinburgh; **St. Bride's,** Bothwell, near Glasgow (1398); **Seton,** East Lothian (1492) (A.M.); **Trinity College Church,** Edinburgh (1460); **Tulliebardine Church,** Perthshire (1446) (A.M.); **Rosslyn Chapel,** Midlothian; **Crichton,** Midlothian; **Dunglass,** East Lothian (1451) (A.M.).

Parish churches
St. Mahew's Chapel, Kirkton, Dumbartonshire (1467 and later); **Borthwick Church,** Midlothian; **Fowlis Easter Church,** Angus.

Burgh churches
St. Giles Church, Edinburgh; **St. Michael's Church,** Linlithgow; **St. Mary's Church,** Haddington (14th–15th c.) (A.M.); **St. Nicholas,** Aberdeen; **Holy Rude Church,** Stirling (15th–16th c.); **Brechin Cathedral,** Angus; **St. John's Church,** Perth.

Abbeys and cathedrals
Crossraguel Abbey, Ayrshire (A.M.); **St. Machar's Cathedral,** Old Aberdeen (A.M.); **Elgin Cathedral,** Morayshire (A.M.); **Dryburgh Abbey,** Berwickshire (A.M.); **Preceptory of the Knights Hospitallers,** Torphichen, West Lothian (A.M.); **Melrose Abbey,** Roxburghshire (A.M.); **Paisley Abbey,** Renfrewshire; **Glasgow Cathedral** (A.M.); **Dunkeld Cathedral,** Perthshire (A.M.).

Bridges
Dervorguilla Bridge, Dumfries; **Stirling Old Bridge** (A.M.).

Further reading

CHILDE, V. GORDON and SIMPSON, W. DOUGLAS *Illustrated Guide to Ancient Monuments* (Vol. VI *Scotland*) Edinburgh, H.M.S.O. 1967

CRUDEN, STEWART *Scottish Abbeys* Edinburgh, H.M.S.O. 1960

CRUDEN, STEWART *The Scottish Castle,* Edinburgh, Nelson, 1963

DUNBAR, JOHN G. *The Historic Architecture of Scotland* London, Batsford 1966

MACKENZIE, W. MACKAY *The Mediaeval Castle in Scotland* London, Methuen 1927

RICHARDSON, JAMES S. *The Mediaeval Stonecarver in Scotland* Edinburgh, University Press 1964

SIMPSON, W. DOUGLAS *Scottish Castles* Edinburgh, H.M.S.O. 1964

Late Decorated Gothic period

Tower-houses

The tower-house was the most representative building of the 15th century and save for changes at the wall-head and internal improvements, continued to be built in substantially the same form as before for most of the period.

Plans continue to show a preference for the rectangular and 'L' type, though there were some variations, e.g. Borthwick Castle, Midlothian.

The external appearance remained severe, though windows were made larger. These were few in number, irregularly placed and made secure with iron grilles. At the wall-head the parapet was now built on open corbels and the corners formed into overhanging open rounds or turrets. The thick walls were finished with dressed stone, or harling over rubble with dressed stone at the corners and around the openings. Roofs were built of slabbed stone or constructed of timber. A guard-room, called a 'cap' house, was situated at a corner to serve the wall-walk. From the wall-head above the entrance it is usual to see an oversailing machicolated parapet which served to guard the door. The entrance was often arched and situated either on the ground floor, or the first floor and reached by a wooden stair.

Internally the tower-house continued to be divided by vaulting, which was either round or pointed, with wooden floors between. Arrangements for greater comfort and privacy included building more chambers within the thickness of the walls as well as passages and newel stairs to serve these. It is not unusual to see a private chapel or oratory included in these arrangements, e.g. at Affleck Castle, Angus. Stone benches flanking the wide window embrasures are common and would have provided a comfortable retreat from an otherwise gloomy and draughty hall.

Staircases were often interrupted, which meant that one had to cross the hall or other principal room in order to climb to a higher level, possibly a consideration of security. The kitchen is sometimes found off the screens passage at the lower end of the hall. Fireplaces, aumbries and panels more commonly received sculptural treatment in the decorative style of the period, and painted decoration is also known. Heraldic devices are introduced in the principal rooms usually on the fireplace wall and occasionally on the outside above the entrance.

Borthwick Castle, Midlothian (1430), viewed from the south-west. One of the outstanding features of this castle is the fine-dressed ashlar masonry with which the external walls are built. The numerous chimneys are an indication of a concern for greater comfort.

Borthwick Castle, Midlothian (1430). Plan of the first floor. Most of the new features introduced into the tower-house appeared in the first half of the 15th century and are well illustrated at Borthwick Castle, which is in a first-class state of preservation and is inhabited.

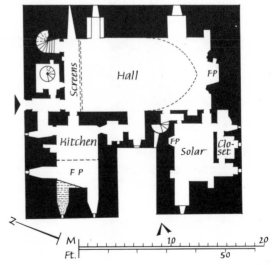

Affleck Castle, Angus, late 15th century. Entrance front. Notice the rounded entrance in the re-entrant angle and above it the recess for an armorial device. At the wall-head a machicolated parapet guards the entrance from above.

Affleck Castle viewed from the south-west. On the ground floor in the middle of the wall appear inverted gunloops of the 'key-hole' type, typical of the latter part of the century.

When more peaceful and prosperous conditions prevailed, the same features began to appear in the smaller towers.

Affleck Castle, section viewed from the north.

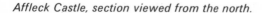

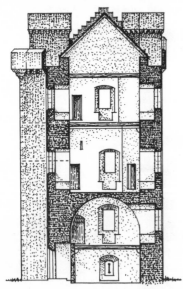

Affleck Castle, plans of ground and third floors.

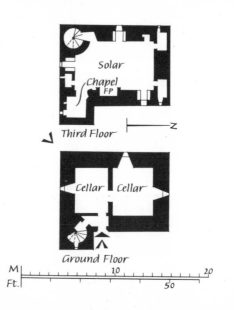

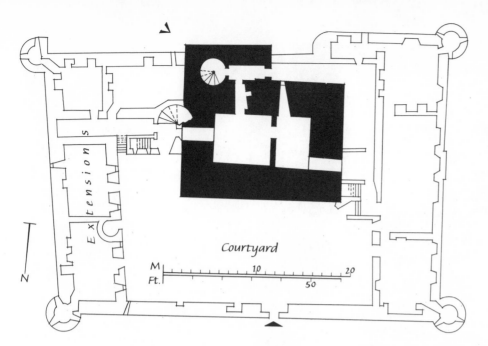

Craigmillar Castle (plan).

Craigmillar Castle, Edinburgh, illustrates how the need for additional accommodation was sometimes met by attaching buildings to the original tower. These often formed a courtyard.

Craigmillar Castle, viewed from the south-east.

View of a tower-house roof showing the parapet wall supported on open corbels and the open turrets overhanging the corners. Access to the wall walk is from the garret. Huntingtower Castle, Perthshire (late 15th century and early 16th century).

A newel stair. Falkland Palace, Fife.

Royal castles and palaces

The exterior of Linlithgow Palace presents a fairly plain appearance although its domestic features predominate over those of defence. One is left in no doubt about the origin of the corner towers and the machicolated wall head.

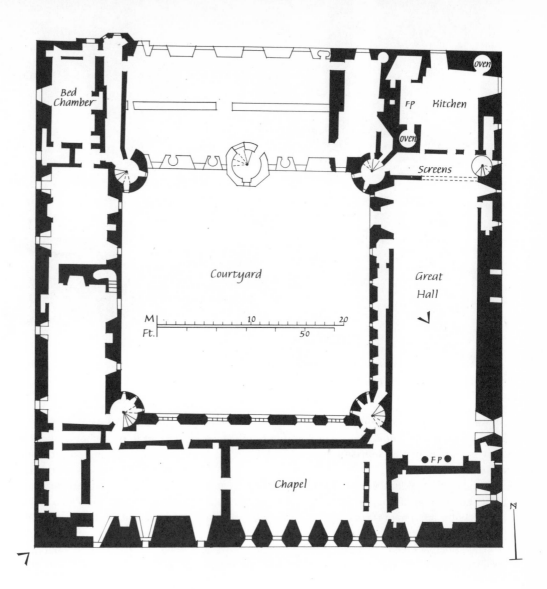

Linlithgow Palace.
Plan of the first floor.

Bed Chamber

oven

FP   Kitchen

oven

Screens

Courtyard

M   10   20
Ft.   50

Great Hall

FP

Chapel

N

Linlithgow Palace, West Lothian, viewed from the south-west.

Linlithgow Palace, the Great Hall or 'Lyon Chalmer'.

Although no royal work started in the 15th century remains complete, some idea of its former magnificence can be got from the substantial remains of Linlithgow Palace.

The present building was started in 1425 and by the time of its completion in 1539 it had assumed a quadrangular form, with apartments arranged on four sides of an open court.

The principal chambers were on the first floor above a vaulted basement and communication was by newel stairs in the four inner corners of the courtyard. Though some apartments opened off corridors others were reached by passing through one room to another.

This compact plan contrasts with the random arrangements in early medieval castles when the hall, chapel and kitchen occupied separate buildings, as for instance in Kildrummy Castle (13th century).

The great Hall or 'Lyon Chalmer' of Linlithgow Palace still displays some of its former grandeur. It was built in the late Gothic style and roofed with an open timber roof of hammer-beam construction, 100 feet (33 metres) long and 30 feet (10 metres) wide. It was lit by clerestory windows between which were statues supported on stone brackets. The hooded fireplace is divided into three compartments by moulded piers. At the opposite end was the 'screens' leading to the kitchen. The walls were finished with a thin layer of plaster and against these were hung tapestries. Painted wall decoration and wood panelling are also known to have existed in the Palace. The stone floors were covered with rushes which was common practice in medieval times.

Church buildings

Apart from the completing or repairing of large cathedrals and abbeys, no religious houses of any size had been erected in Scotland since the early part of the 14th century.

Building was limited almost entirely to parish churches and a distinctive kind called collegiate churches. They were erected and endowed by wealthy landowners and served by a college or small body of secular clergy who, by the deed of foundation, had to sing masses for the soul of the founder and others named by him. They had few or no parochial commitments.

These churches make a significant contribution to the ecclesiastical architecture of Scotland in the 15th and first part of the 16th centuries, a contribution which can be likened to that of the king and great nobles who founded the abbeys and monasteries in the 12th and 13th centuries. Other endowments took the form of chantries and chapels in existing large churches.

A drawing showing the parts of a small medieval church with the fabric cut open.

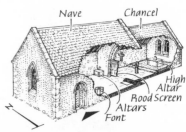

Collegiate churches often occupied an old sacred site (e.g. Seton), or formed an enlargement of an existing parish church, and were usually situated near the castle of the founder (e.g. Kirkton, Dumbartonshire).

Seton Collegiate Church, East Lothian, is a typical example of the collegiate building. It was started about 1470 and continued with interruptions until late in the 16th century. Such interrupted building activity, unfinished in spite of its small size, was common.

Like so many collegiate churches, it was planned as an aisleless cruciform, i.e. as a single chamber with a crossing (others adopted the rectangular plan of the simple parish church). In this church only the chancel, choir, sacristy and transepts surmounted with a tower and truncated broach spire were completed before building stopped.

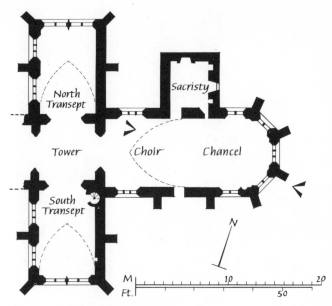

Seton Collegiate Church (plan).

Typical features of the late Pointed Gothic style in Scotland illustrated by Seton are the preference for curvilinear window tracery, the three-sided termination of the apse, the stone-slabbed roof and the blank east transept walls.

Seton Collegiate Church, Interior of chancel.

The interior of Seton Collegiate Church illustrates the high pointed barrel vault so typical of late Scottish Medieval architecture. This is decorated with moulded ribs which enhance the chancel but serve no structural purpose.

In true rib and panel vaulting the ribs form an integral part of the construction. The solid barrel vault is self-supporting, if the walls are of sufficent thickness to withstand the weight and outward thrust of the heavy vault. At Seton, and in many other churches, the walls were pierced with large windows and they were reduced in thickness and strength. Thus it was necessary to build substantial buttresses between the windows to give additional support.

The height of the window was also restricted by this type of vaulting, which is perhaps one of the reasons for retaining the Decorated style window tracery. It is worth remembering that in England at this time the Decorated style had given way to a Perpendicular form, a fine early example of which is seen at Melrose Abbey. On the Continent, on the other hand, and notably in France, the Decorated style evolved into a Flamboyant form and it was possibly this source which helped to inspire Scottish masons at this time.

The combined effect, then, of the high pointed barrel vault, roofed with heavy stone slabs, the comparatively low windows with pronounced buttresses protruding between them and the preference for Decorated style window tracery is most characteristic of this period in Scotland. It shows an admirable solution to the problems of the Gothic, with features borrowed from England and abroad, in a country less prosperous. It was this kind of ingenuity, seen also in the tower-house, which was so typical of the work of Scottish masons from the middle 15th to the 17th century and culminated in a national style.

With a return of some measure of prosperity in the 15th century, some burghs rebuilt and enlarged their churches. They were generally fairly large aisled and cruciform buildings with a tower at the crossing, or at one end, e.g. St. Michael's Church, Linlithgow. Some towns, following the example of the landed proprietors, had their churches elevated to collegiate status, with merchant burgesses and craftsmen founding chaplainries and altars within the church, e.g. St. Giles, Edinburgh.

St. Michael's Church, Linlithgow (plan).

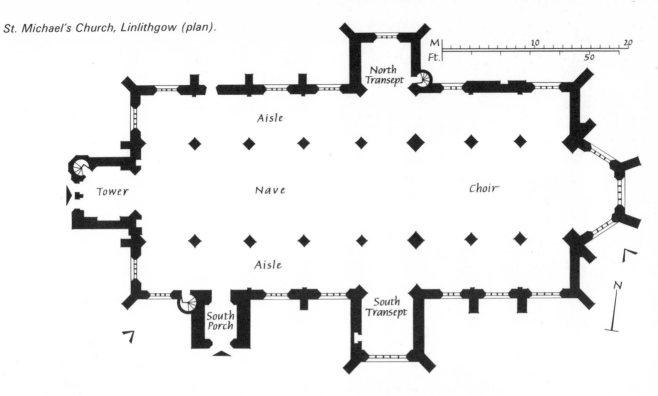

St. Michael's Church, Linlithgow. Features from castellated and domestic architecture make their appearance in churches in the form of crenellated parapets, round towers with conical roofs, crow-stepped gables and stepped buttresses. Notice the clerestory windows which have reverted to the semi-circular arch, and the two styles of Gothic window tracery.

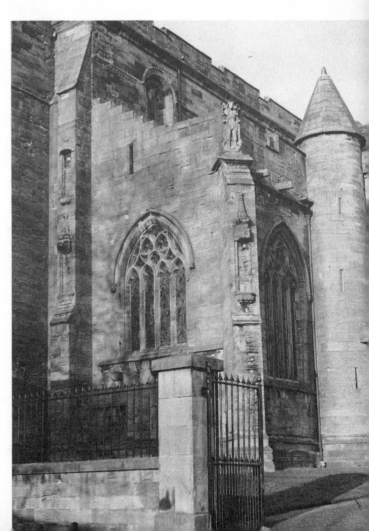

Dryburgh Abbey, Berwickshire. The reintroduction of the round arch for doors and windows was a usual feature at this time, though the carved moulding was of Gothic character. The 15th century west doorway to the nave of Dryburgh Abbey illustrates this. The dressed facing stones have been removed, revealing the rubble core. A derelict building was commonly regarded as a good quarry by later builders!

Bridges

In Scotland, where so much of the country is mountainous and the lowlands are divided by rivers, bridges are important. Early bridges were narrow and spanned the river in a series of elliptical or semi-circular arches carried on heavy piers which have pointed cut-waters. At intervals along the parapet wall recesses were built to allow pedestrians to stand aside while traffic passed by.

Dervorguilla Bridge, Dumfries.

8 Sixteenth Century

James IV (1488–1513); James V (1513–42); Mary 'Queen of Scots' (1542–67); James VI (1567–1625).

The religious and political upheavals of this century left Scotland a Protestant country, but with the king and nobles favouring episcopacy, while the lesser barons, lairds and merchants favoured presbyterianism. This led to bitter struggles in the 17th century. The Reformed Church strove to implement the proposals of the Book of Discipline which was concerned with the payment of ministers, the establishment of a school in every parish and the care of the poor, but they were hindered by lack of money.

Even before the Reformation, much church property had fallen into the hands of laymen. The church itself had feued out land to meet the heavy demands of taxation and the king had granted monasteries and abbeys to people with little or no monastic connections. It was impossible for the government or the Reformed Church to recover these properties, and the buildings, many already decaying because of lack of money or English raids, were not restored by their new owners.

Economically Scotland was still a poor country with a primitive system of agriculture. Food was simple and often insufficient, clothing was home-spun and sanitation was almost non-existent. Roads between towns were no more than beaten tracks, frequently impassable. A cart road existed between Edinburgh and Glasgow and one or two other centres, but vehicular traffic was rare. Transport was confined to the pack-horse and coasting craft. The wealthier merchants could import luxuries to make their houses more comfortable, but the barons' and lairds' houses, in the main, and even the Palace of Holyrood-house, were sparsely furnished, though built of dressed stone.

The east coast burghs traded with France, the Low Countries, England and the Baltic, the west coast with England, France and Ireland. The main exports were wool, skins, smoked or dried fish and coarse cloth, while the main imports were iron, timber for building, pitch, tar, wine, fine cloths and a few luxuries.

The six leading burghs were Aberdeen, Dundee, Edinburgh, Glasgow, Perth and St. Andrews. Of these, Edinburgh, using the port of Leith, was by far the wealthiest, noted for the large number of fine buildings within its walls. The first printing press with movable type in Scotland was set up in Edinburgh in the early part of the century. The burghs were not large; few had a population of more than two thousand, most had only a few hundred.

In burghs and country districts alike, breaches of the peace were common, despite the sovereign's attempts to enforce law and order. In the Highlands and in the Borders, poor communications made lawlessness even worse.

Building activity

From the closing years of the 15th century to 1560 there was less building in Scotland, with the notable exception of the royal works. After the Reformation, 1560, there was a renewed interest in building generally, particularly of tower-houses and mansion houses. Pre-Reformation churches were modified to meet the needs of the Reformed Church, otherwise little church building was carried out.

Most building was now in stone, although in burghs timber houses continued to be built, despite the obvious fire risk. For lesser buildings in the country a variety of materials and methods were employed and these showed local variations.

Architectural character

The king introduced the Renaissance style to Scotland in the rebuilding of the royal castles and palaces, but this did not affect architecture in general. After the Reformation there was a resumption of traditional forms. The tower-house enters its third and last phase with increasing concessions to comfort and the open mansion house begins to develop from the tower-house, which is indicative of more peaceful times with a greater measure of prosperity.

The earliest examples of burgh architecture date from the 16th century and they are in a style which remained traditional. In church architecture Gothic forms persisted and vernacular mannerisms are widely in evidence.

Buildings to see
Royal castles and palaces which show early Renaissance influence
Stirling Castle, Stirlingshire (A.M.); **Linlithgow Palace,** West Lothian (A.M.); **Falkland Palace,** Fife (N.T.S.); **Edinburgh Castle,** the Great Hall (A.M.).

Medieval courtyard arrangements, some with features not representative of Scottish architecture as a whole

Craignethan Castle, Lanarkshire (*c.* 1530–40) (A.M.); Drochil Castle, Peeblesshire (*c.* 1578); Crichton Castle, Midlothian (1581–92) (courtyard façade) (A.M.); Tolquhon Castle, Aberdeenshire (1584–9) (A.M.); Boyne Castle, Banffshire (late 16th c.); Edzell Castle, Angus (16th and 17th c.) (A.M.).

Castles which show a development towards the open mansion house
Elcho Castle, Perthshire (*c.* 1580) (A.M.); Castle Menzies, Perthshire (1571–77); Huntly Castle, Aberdeenshire (1597–1606) (A.M.); Kilmartin Castle, Argyll (late 16th c.); Ferniehirst Castle, Roxburghshire; Prestongrange, East Lothian; Melgund Castle, Angus; Torwoodhead Castle, Stirlingshire (1566); Carnasserie Castle, Argyll (A.M.); Newark Castle, Renfrewshire (A.M.); Muchalls Castle, Kincardineshire; Drochil Castle, Peeblesshire (1570–80); Maclellan's Castle, Kirkcudbrightshire (1582) (A.M.); Huntingtower, Perthshire (15th and 16th c.) (A.M.); Lauriston Castle, Edinburgh (late 16th c.); Luffness House, East Lothian (late 16th c.); Linhouse, Midlothian (*c.* 1589); Muness Castle, Shetland (1598) (A.M.); Traquair House, Peeblesshire (15th and 16th c.).

Tower-house (rectangular)
Corgarff Castle, Aberdeenshire (A.M.); Smailholm Tower, Roxburghshire (A.M.); Towie Barclay, Aberdeenshire; Hallbar Tower, Lanarkshire (*c.* 1581); Lochhouse Tower, Dumfriesshire; Cakemuir House, Midlothian.

Tower-house ('L' plan)
Greenknowe Tower, Berwickshire (1581) (A.M.); Fiddes Castle, Kincardineshire (late 16th c.); Crathes Castle, Aberdeenshire (1596) (N.T.S.); Balbegno Castle, Kincardineshire (1569); Rosyth Castle, Fife (A.M.); Brackie Castle, Angus (1581).

Tower-house ('Z' plan)
Claypotts Castle, Angus (1569–88) (A.M.); Glenbuchart Castle, Aberdeenshire (1590) (A.M.); Midmar Castle, Aberdeenshire (*c.* 1570); Terpersie Castle, Aberdeenshire (1561); Noltland Castle, Isle of Westray, Orkney (A.M.).

Churches
St. Serf's, Dysart, Fife; Grandtully Chapel, Perthshire (*c.* 1533) (A.M.); Holy Rude Church, Stirling (15th and 16th c.); St. Machar's Cathedral, Old Aberdeen; The Chapel Royal, Stirling (1594) (A.M.); Aytoun Church, Berwickshire; Anstruther Wester, Fife; Blair Church, Perthshire; St. Columba's Church, Burntisland, Fife (1592); Chapel, Hailes Castle, East Lothian (A.M.); Kemback Church, Fife (1587); St. Bean's Church, Perthshire; Weem Church, Perthshire; St. Magridin's Church, Abdie, Fife; The Magdalen Chapel, Edinburgh.

Burgh architecture
Little Houses, Culross, Fife (N.T.S.); Huntly House, Edinburgh (1570); John Knox's House, Edinburgh.

Further reading

APTED, M. R. *The Painted Ceilings of Scotland 1550–1650* Edinburgh, H.M.S.O. 1966
CHILDE, V. GORDON and SIMPSON, W. DOUGLAS *Illustrated Guide to Ancient Monuments* (Vol. VI Scotland) Edinburgh, H.M.S.O. 1967
CRUDEN, STEWART *The Scottish Castle* Edinburgh, Nelson 1963
DUNBAR, JOHN G. *The Historic Architecture of Scotland* London, Batsford 1966
HAY, GEORGE *The Architecture of Scottish Post-Reformation Churches 1560–1843* Oxford, Clarendon Press 1957
MACKENZIE, W. MACKAY *The Mediaeval Castle in Scotland* London, Metheun 1927
RICHARDSON, JAMES S. *The Mediaeval Stonecarver in Scotland* Edinburgh, University Press 1964
SIMPSON, W. DOUGLAS *Scottish Castles* Edinburgh H.M.S.O. 1964

Late Gothic and Scottish Vernacular

Early Renaissance influence

The rebuilding of the royal castles and palaces which began at the end of the 15th century continued during the 16th century. This was not because of a need for defence, but to meet demands for greater comfort and splendour inspired by the Renaissance then fashionable among the nobility in Western Europe.

The Renaissance style of design, which originated in Italy, appeared in France in the beginning of the 16th century, whence it was introduced to Scotland by the king. This was at a time of close diplomatic relations between the two countries. French master masons were brought to Scotland in connection with the royal works.

Two outstanding examples which illustrate the influence of Renaissance design are the courtyard façade of the South Range of Falkland Palace and the Palace of Stirling Castle. Both date from about 1540.

The courtyard façade of the south range of Falkland Palace bears a close resemblance to the early Renaissance style of the royal palaces in France of this time. The façade is grafted on to an earlier building and makes a striking contrast to the street façade (not illustrated) which is of late Gothic design.

The palace block at Stirling Castle, though Renaissance in conception and also of French influence, retains traces of late Gothic, notably in the cusped arches over the carved figures and in the crenellated parapet.

Tower-houses

Between 1560 and the 1630s the tower-house enjoyed a new phase of popularity. The lesser gentry, many of whom had come into possession of church lands, chose to build tower-houses for themselves rather than ordinary houses, perhaps because of the social cachet attached to the former.

Since there was no longer such a need for defence, a number of new features appear in response to a desire for privacy, comfort and baronial display. The upper part, no longer required as a fighting platform, was developed for additional accommodation.

The traditional rectangular and 'L' type plans remained most popular and were further developed within the limitations which these types imposed. But the desire for increased accommodation without departing from the tower-house proper resulted in the introduction of yet another type, the 'Z'. This was formed by the addition of towers at two diagonally opposite corners of the rectangular plan. This arrangement also improved security since all the outside walls of the main block were overlooked.

Defensive features which were retained were the severely plain walls, broken only by well-barred windows, strategically placed shot-holes in window sills, corbels

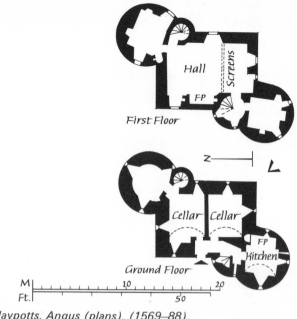

Claypotts, Angus (plans). (1569–88).

Claypotts, Angus, viewed from the south-east.

Huntingtower Castle, Perthshire, showing a method of construction for floors and ceilings. This decoration is the earliest surviving example, c. 1540. Remnants of wall plaster and painting can be seen in this picture.

and walls, and in some an observation hole in a window-sill or a machicolated platform immediately above the entrance. The simple entrance was closed with a heavy oak door secured with a draw-bar and an iron yett.

A panel with the owner's device, initials and date of building is often seen above the entrance. Round turrets and square projections resting on finely made corbels containing stairways or small rooms start at various heights on the angles of the building and continue up beyond the roof-line, sometimes enclosing the gable-end completely.

The main internal arrangements remained much the same but with some increased concessions to comfort. Additional rooms in the upper part of the house with private access resulted in a remarkable number of rooms being crowded in a comparatively small plan. Decoration in the principal rooms consisted of wooden panelling, sometimes painted, and moulded plaster ceilings. Floors of wood or stone were covered with grasses and strewn with sweet-smelling herbs. Furniture was simple and locally made or imported, consisting of a chair or two for the laird, trestle tables, benches, kists and box-beds.

A barmkin wall forming a courtyard surrounded the tower-house at this late date. At Craigievar (17th century) there is part of the original wall with its entrance and a circular angle tower. Within the barmkin wall were stables and other buildings. Outside the wall stood the dovecot, frequently circular up to this time, but later often built with lean-to roof or gabled. (See pages 62 and 77).

The plans of the ground and first floor of Claypotts illustrate the advantages which the 'Z' type layout provided. The projecting corner towers made possible private rooms larger than the cramped wall-chambers of the earlier tower-houses. It will be noticed that the walls of the hall are thinner. This was because it was more usual for all floors above this level to be of timber. The thick walls were necessary in earlier towers to withstand the heavy stone vaults.

Main stairways tended to be wider and were sometimes built in one of the towers. (See Elcho page 62). Usually short flights of newel stairs from the hall served private apartments in the upper stories.

In the lower walls provision was made for hand guns in the form of wide-mouthed shot-holes which were first introduced at the beginning of the century. Often these served little more purpose than to give a show of strength. In many examples of late castellated architecture they are altogether absent or treated in a decorative manner.

Larger windows are common, shuttered in the lower half and glazed in the upper half, and made secure with iron grilles. (The sash windows in Claypotts are modern.)

In the upper stories the corbelled wall-walk and corner turrets were often replaced by a tiled roof extending to the outside walls. Domestic features such as dormer windows and large chimneys rising from crow-stepped gables are common in late castellated architecture.

Balbegno Castle, Kincardineshire (1569), viewed from the south-east, illustrates clearly how former defensive features at the top of the tower have been built over to form additional rooms.

Mansion houses

From the third quarter of the 16th century we see the beginning of a development from the tower house to the mansion house. Many of these retained much of the overall external appearance of the tower-house, but provided the owner with considerably more commodious accommodation. This was often done by extending the plan of the main block lengthwise, which then assumed a form recalling the earlier hall house.

The main part of the building contained the hall with a solar leading off it over a vaulted undercroft which contained the kitchen and cellarage. Sometimes above the hall were private chambers usually reached separately by private stairs. The numerous chimney stacks and the increase in the size of the windows were typical of the time and emphasise the new concern for domesticity.

Defensive features on the wall-head became less pronounced though they did not disappear altogether. A few wide-mouthed shot-holes were placed in the lower wall faces and for outer defences there were sometimes an enclosing barmkin and a ditch.

The houses varied in size and amenity according to the wealth of their owners. Variations of plan formed by incorporating projecting towers or wings to the main longitudinal block produced traditional types, such as the 'L', 'T' and 'Z' plans. There are others of irregular plan.

Earlier existing tower-houses were altered to provide greater accommodation on the lines of the mansion house, e.g. Huntingtower, Perthshire, and Traquair House, Peeblesshire (page 64).

A circular dovecot at Dirleton Castle, East Lothian.

Elcho Castle, Perthshire (1570–80). The plan illustrates the extended main block with the hall and solar on the first floor. The main staircase occupies the lower part of the largest tower. Its wide graceful rise was a feature which began to be more generally introduced.

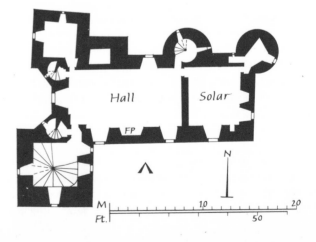

Elcho Castle, Perthshire. The exterior south front illustrates the predominance of domestic features over defensive in the size of the windows and the numerous chimneystacks. Above the hall were two floors of private rooms. The roof of the main block is of timber and slate and extends to the wall-head, broken only with dormer windows and an enclosed turret. The stair tower retains the wall walk behind a crenellated parapet with roofed turrets projecting from the corners for the watchman.

Elcho Castle, Perthshire. Detail of the roof of the main block illustrating the dormer windows and the round turret with its conical roof. The carved window-surrounds form almost the only external decorative features. The 'domesticated' projecting corner turret is an architectural feature which is characteristic of late Scottish castellated architecture. Compare this view with Huntingtower, Perthshire, and Drum Castle, Aberdeenshire, to see how it developed.

Traquair House, near Innerleithen, Peeblesshire, viewed from the entrance front.

Traquair is a very fine example of a 15–16th century mansion house which has been developed from a tower-house into its present form by additions, and has been continuously occupied. The service wings, screen wall and gateway were built by James Smith between 1695 and 1705.

Church buildings

Up to the Reformation the form of church building followed the same lines as those of the previous century. Romanesque and Gothic features combine with late castellated features to form a national style in church building, which in many cases was picturesque if at times lacking in good proportions.

The English Perpendicular style of Gothic rarely achieved the same subtlety in Scotland, where the Decorated style was preferred.

King's College Chapel, Aberdeen (1500–1506), viewed from the west. This is a typical example of the late Gothic style in Scotland. The crown steeple is one of three surviving examples; the others are at Tolbooth, Glasgow, and St. Giles, Edinburgh. There were crown steeples in several other places at this time, although they were not common. The stepped buttresses, crow-stepped gables and florid window tracery, which can be seen under pointed and round arches, are all fairly typical features.

St. Machar's Cathedral, Old Aberdeen. The west front with its twin towers erected about 1530 displays the preference for features from castellated and Romanesque architecture typical of the 15th and 16th centuries.

After the Reformation the internal arrangements in existing churches were altered to meet the needs of the Reformed Church. Congregational worship required only a single chamber building and the subdivisions of nave, chancel, apse, transepts and chapel interfered with this. The smaller parish churches were easily adapted but in larger churches often only part of the building was maintained and the remainder used for other purposes or allowed to fall into decay. In towns large churches were sometimes partitioned to serve more than one parish.

The responsibility for maintaining the church fabric and providing the stipend fell on the local landholder who was often unable or unwilling to do so. Thus both the adapting of existing buildings and the building of new ones were delayed for lack of money. This also had the effect of producing buildings of inferior aesthetic merit.

Post-Reformation parish churches followed the medieval plan of a long rectangle and generally were of the simplest form and plain in appearance. In congregational worship the pulpit usually occupied a place in the middle of the south wall with the baptismal font nearby. In front of the pulpit were placed long communion tables for the celebration of the Lord's Supper.

Seating arrangements were of social significance and varied from church to church. In some, as in St. Magridin's, the local heritor built his own aisle. In addition to the seating on the ground floor there were lofts or galleries. (See page 81.)

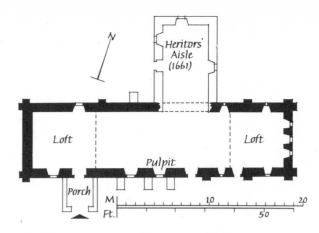

St. Magridin's Church, Abdie, Fife. A 13th century church with post-Reformation alterations.

The Chapel Royal, Stirling Castle, a royal foundation built in 1594, is unusual in its display of early classic Renaissance architecture. This was not to be seen widely until the 18th century.

Burgh architecture

From the 16th century more buildings in the burghs were built of stone but most seem to have incorporated timber for overhanging galleries and extensions, supported on wooden posts or brackets.

Houses were divided internally into a number of self-contained apartments, each consisting of two or three rooms; the main room was the hall with a chamber and sometimes a kitchen. Access to each dwelling was by a common newel stair, though the first floor was often entered by an outside stair. Galleries or balconies extended from various floors which gave the occupants an opportunity of taking the air away from the immediate stench of the streets. The ground floor was taken up with cellarage, shops, workshops or stables.

The rear view of Huntly House illustrates the manner in which medieval buildings grew to meet the demands of their occupants and their situation. This is most characteristic of vernacular architecture. The pend leading through the building to the main street is a typical feature. The rubble walls would have been harled originally.

Huntly House, Edinburgh (1570). The upper floors of this house are of timber construction and plastered over lath. The house has been restored to its original appearance and is now used as a City museum.

Plan forms varied a good deal, though the 'L' and 'T' plans tended to predominate. Irregularities of the site often determined the form of the plan. Height depended on the number of floors, which in congested burghs might be as many as three or four with an attic, though two floors with an attic was more general.

9 Seventeenth Century

James VI and I (1567–1625); Charles I (1625–49); Commonwealth (1649–59); Charles II (1660–85); James VII and II (1685–88); William of Orange (1689–1702).

The geographical extent of Scotland at the Union of the Crowns (1603) was the same as it is to-day. Although the regal union left Scotland with its own government and Church, these were controlled from England by the king. But a strong sense of independence was growing, and the increasingly powerful burgess class resented government through the Privy Council, and the General Assembly of the Church of Scotland, who demanded Presbyterianism, were violently opposed to Episcopacy. In an attempt to impose the English form of worship and doctrine, Charles I made Edinburgh a bishopric with St. Giles as its cathedral church, and gave it formal recognition as the capital. Civil wars and religious persecutions were rife, and these, together with high taxation, poor industrial techniques and feudal farming methods, were responsible for a backward and unprofitable national economy.

The Commonwealth under Cromwell provided a respite, although toleration of all Protestant sects did not meet with approval from the Presbyterians. Life and property were safe and trade was free between Scotland and England. Heavy taxation to maintain military establishments such as the large forts at Leith, Ayr, Perth, Inverlochy and Inverness, almost ruined the country.

Before and after the Commonwealth, the Crown, and many nobles and lairds enriched by grants of former church estates, tried to improve industry and commerce, but they were resisted by burgesses of the royal burghs, who shortsightedly insisted on their monopolies. Many nobles and lairds, however, went into business on their own account, trading through the burghs of barony, many of which grew up during this time.

Overseas trade affected the fortune of the country as a whole. The practice of exporting raw materials at a low price and importing costly manufactured goods was a drain on the country's economy which legislation did little to stop. Glasgow was exceptional in that it increasingly pioneered trade with America, importing raw materials and re-exporting the finished product. Its increased prosperity and many fine new buildings were noted by travellers of the time.

Despite political and ecclesiastical strife, considerable constitutional progress was made in the system of local administration by shire, parish and burgh. Statutory force was given to the ideal of an elementary school in every parish, bequeathed by the early reformers, and a good many were established. The large burghs had schools for secondary education and there were five universities—St. Andrews; Glasgow; King's, Aberdeen; Edinburgh; Marischal, Aberdeen. Learned societies received Royal Charters and the foundations of modern Scots law were laid.

Building activity
Conditions in the country after the Reformation had created an atmosphere suitable to building which was intensified after the Union of the Crowns. The lairds' newly-acquired wealth from church lands and trade resulted in renewed building activity in the latter half of the 16th century which continued well into the 17th century. As well as the building of new castles, old ones were made more comfortable by the addition of rooms with private access and decoration in the new style. Social unrest and economic factors, however, had the effect of causing the completion of buildings to be protracted. In the burghs, houses were being built with their fronts of stone instead of wood. The dwellings of the common people were mostly still very primitive constructions of rough stone, clay or turf, spanned by wood trusses, thatched with heather or straw, where the smoke found its way out through a hole in the roof—such is the 'black house', of which the last remains are to be seen in the Hebrides today.

Architectural character
The medieval tradition lasted for a long time in Scotland because of the country's remoteness, lack of wealth and unsettled state of government. One of the signs of an increase in prosperity after the Reformation and particularly after the Union of the Crowns was the introduction of Renaissance motifs applied decoratively to traditional forms. The new style originated in Italy in the 15th century and came to Scotland via the Low Countries, England, France and Germany through trade connections and imported pattern books. The chief exponent of the style was William Wallace, principal master mason to the Crown from 1617–31, who thereby helped to prepare the way for the classical school in Scotland. The interpretation of the new forms by local masons trained in tradi-

tional forms of design resulted in a transitional style peculiar to Scotland. The term Scottish Baronial is often applied to this style, the last phase of castellated architecture in Scotland, e.g., Craigievar Castle, Aberdeenshire. Buildings planned in the shape of the letter 'L' and modifications of this, continued as a favourite layout for town and country houses well into the century. The classical style, evolved by Inigo Jones in England, was introduced to Scotland late in the century in the mansion houses. These followed the example of the Palace of Holyroodhouse redesigned by Sir William Bruce, who is regarded as the principal exponent of this classical school in Scotland.

Buildings to see

Tower-houses (rectangular plan)
Amisfield Tower, Dumfriesshire (1600); **Repentance Tower,** Dumfriesshire; **Spedlin's Tower,** Dumfriesshire (1605 and earlier); **Coxton Tower,** Morayshire (1644); **Aldie Castle,** Kinross-shire.

Tower-houses ('L' plan)
Craigievar Castle, Aberdeenshire (1626) (N.T.S.); **Crathes Castle,** Kincardineshire (16th and 17th c.) (N.T.S.); **Scotstarvet Tower,** Fife (1627) (A.M.); **Scalloway Castle,** Shetland (1600) (A.M.); **Leslie Castle,** Aberdeenshire (1661); **Elshieshields Tower,** Dumfriesshire; **Castle Leod,** Ross and Cromarty (c. 1616); **Lethendy Castle,** Perthshire (1678).

Castles and mansions which show affinities with the tower-house
Castle Stewart, Inverness-shire (1625); **Huntly Castle,** Aberdeenshire (17th c. and earlier) (A.M.); **Fyvie Castle,** Aberdeenshire (1600); **Craigston Castle,** Aberdeenshire (1605); **Leith Hall,** Kennethmont, Aberdeenshire (N.T.S.); **Glamis Castle,** Angus (17th c. and earlier); **Huntingtower Castle,** Perthshire (15th–17th centuries) (A.M.); **Northfield House,** Prestonpans, East Lothian (1611); **Winton House,** East Lothian (c. 1620); **Innes House,** Morayshire (c. 1650).

Town houses
Argyll's Lodging, Stirling; **The Palace,** Culross, Fife (A.M.); **Moray House,** Edinburgh; **Acheson House,** Edinburgh (1633); **Lamb's House,** Leith; **Maclellan's House,** Kirkcudbright (A.M.); **Provost Skene's House,**

Aberdeen (17th c. and earlier); **Provost Ross's House,** Aberdeen; **Old Hamilton House,** Prestonpans, East Lothian (1628).

Early Scottish Renaissance houses
Earl Patrick's Palace, Kirkwall, Orkney (c. 1600) (A.M.); **Drumlanrig Castle,** Dumfriesshire (1675–89); **Hopetoun House,** West Lothian (1699–1702); **Kinross House,** Kinross-shire (c. 1686–91); **Melville House,** Ladybank, Fife (1696–1701); **Nithsdale Building,** Caerlaverock Castle, Dumfriesshire (1634) (A.M.); **George Heriot's Hospital,** Edinburgh (1627–50); **The Palace of Holyroodhouse,** Edinburgh (1671) (A.M.); **Caroline Park,** Edinburgh.

Churches
Lyne, Peeblesshire (c. 1645); **Lauder,** Berwickshire (1673); **Cawdor,** Nairnshire; **Alloa,** Clackmannanshire (the steeple) (1680); **Walston,** Lanarkshire (1656); **Anstruther Easter,** Fife (1634 and 1644); **Tulliallan,** Fife (1675); **Dairsie,** Fife (1621); **Fordell Chapel,** Fife (1650); **Greyfriars,** Edinburgh (1638 and later); **Canongate,** Edinburgh (1688).

Burgh architecture
Culross, Fife; **Anstruther Easter,** Fife; **Inverkeithing,** Fife; **Falkland,** Fife; **St. Andrews,** Fife; **Elgin,** Morayshire; **Kirkcudbright; Kirkwall,** Orkney; **Haddington,** East Lothian; **Aberdeen; Stirling; Edinburgh.**

Further reading
APTED, M. R. *The Painted Ceilings of Scotland 1550–1650* Edinburgh, H.M.S.O. 1966
CHILDE, V. GORDON and SIMPSON, W. DOUGLAS *Illustrated Guide to Ancient Monuments* (Vol. VI *Scotland*) Edinburgh, H.M.S.O. 1967
CRUDEN, STEWART *The Scottish Castle* Edinburgh, Nelson 1963
DUNBAR, JOHN G. *The Historic Architecture of Scotland* London, Batsford 1966
HAY, GEORGE *The Architecture of Scottish Post-Reformation Churches 1560–1843* Oxford, Clarendon Press 1957
SCOTT-MONCRIEFF, GEORGE (Editor) *The Stones of Scotland* London, Batsford 1938
SIMPSON, W. DOUGLAS *Scottish Castles* Edinburgh, H.M.S.O. 1964

Early Scottish Renaissance

Until about 1660 the Renaissance style had made its appearance mainly in the form of decorative embellishments to such things as fireplaces, windows and armorial panels. These were executed according to the ingenuity of the medieval master mason working from imported pattern books from England, the Netherlands and elsewhere. It became incorporated into the vernacular style, and through its interpretation achieved a character peculiarly its own. William Wallace, principal master mason to the Crown from 1617 until his death in 1631, was the chief exponent of this kind of decoration and was widely copied.

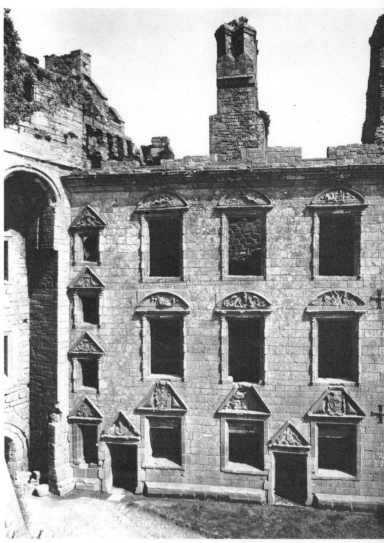

Nithsdale's Building (c. 1634) a mansion built within the courtyard of the ancient stronghold of Caerlaverock Castle, Dumfriesshire, is a good example of early Renaissance in Scotland.

The entrance to Argyll's Lodging, Stirling (1632), illustrating the prevailing fashion for decorating the window heads, armorial panels and entrance with strap-work and neo-classical details. Originally the windows on the ground floor were much smaller, and there was no gutter across the dormer windows.

Courtyard houses

The transition from the late Scottish castellated to the Renaissance style is illustrated in two important buildings, George Heriot's Hospital, Edinburgh, a boys' school, and Drumlanrig Castle, Dumfriesshire, a ducal mansion. They are designed in the form of a square enclosing a courtyard, typical of mature Renaissance plans inspired by Italian and French architecture. They differ from earlier courtyard plans because they were designed in this way in the first place, and did not assume this form by later additions, e.g., Linlithgow Palace.

These two buildings retain a number of features which remind us of Scottish castellated architecture, e.g., the pronounced corner 'towers' and round turrets at the wall-head. At the same time they display the Renaissance style in the form of a symmetrical layout and orderly arrangement of windows and doors, and the addition of decorative details of a classical origin which was as yet foreign to Scotland. This is clearly seen in the entrance front of Drumlanrig Castle, while elsewhere this building retains traditional Scottish features.

The application of classical details was not properly understood, but the total effect combined with persisting castellated features is picturesque, typical of Scottish architecture of this period, and a source of inspiration to architects of the 19th century. Drumlanrig is one of the first houses to have corridors incorporated as an essential part of the plan.

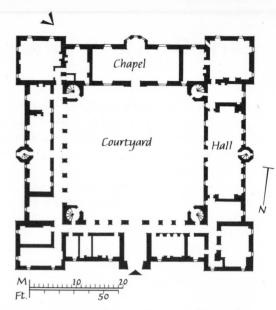

George Heriot's Hospital, Edinburgh, ground floor plan.

George Heriot's Hospital, Edinburgh, (1627–50), seen from the south-east. Begun in 1627 by William Wallace and completed about 1650 by William Ayton.

Drumlanrig Castle, Dumfriesshire (1675–89). (?) Designed by James Smith (d. 1731). Entrance front.

Drumlanrig Castle. Plan of the first floor.

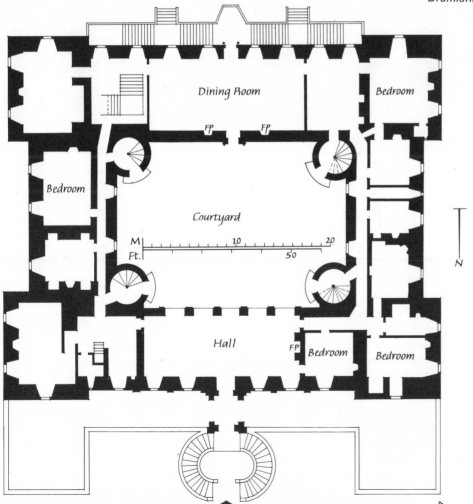

The courtyard of the Palace of Holyroodhouse begun in 1671 by Sir William Bruce, showing the mature classical style in the proportions of the elevation and correct use of detail.

Originating in Italy in the early 15th century the Renaissance style spread throughout the continent wherever conditions were favourable to its development. By the beginning of the 17th century England possessed many fine Elizabethan mansions in a transitional style. In Scotland Barnes Castle, East Lothian (1594) (uncompleted) and the Earl's Palace, Kirkwall (c. 1600) are the only comparable works. By 1616 Inigo Jones had evolved the classical style in England. It was not until the latter half of this century that this mature classical style made its appearance in Scotland through the work of the Surveyor-General for Scotland, Sir William Bruce of Kinross (c. 1630–1710).

Tower-houses

The last phase of castellated architecture in Scotland continued well into the 17th century. Features of a defensive origin were turned to decorative effect, more noticeably so on the upper walls. The staggered corbel string-course suggestive of machicolation, and mock cannon sometimes serving as water spouts, are examples of this. Another typical feature was the introduction of Renaissance forms. These are to be seen as decoration on pedimented dormers, armorial panels and fireplaces. The interpretation of the new forms with traditional features by native masons was often both bold and harmonious.

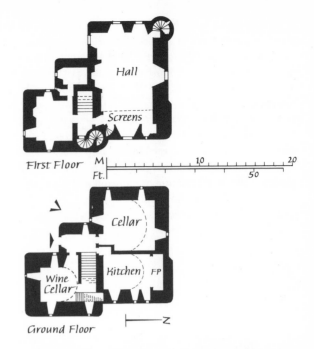

Craigievar Castle, Aberdeenshire (1626), seen from the south-west. This fine tower-house, without additions, stands today as it was completed. A barmkin wall with angle towers surrounded the castle, part of this can still be seen on the left of the picture.

Craigievar Castle, Aberdeenshire. Ground and first floor plans. A modified 'L' plan with the entrance in the re-entrant angle. As well as the straight stair to the first floor, there is a narrow stair leading from the hall to the wine cellar.

Timber floors over the hall were more common by this time, although the hall at Craigievar is stone-vaulted. The illustration shows the original wooden screen with the door in the centre and musicians' galleries above, which are medieval features. The small square aumbry in the fireplace is an important detail found in every house, and was used for storing salt. Aumbries or wall cupboards are commonly found in tower-houses and were furnished with wooden shelves and closed with wooden doors. The carving of the wooden panelling round the wall, the moulded plaster decoration of the vault and the enormous coat of arms above the fireplace are typical of this time and illustrate the taste for Renaissance decoration.

Stone-vaulted hall, Craigievar Castle (from a drawing by Robert Billings).

Detail of Amisfield Tower illustrating the 'domestic' development that took place around the upper floors. The decorative enrichments to windows, gable ends and corner turrets derive from medieval and Renaissance sources. The built-out dormer rising from corbels is provided with an observation hole in the sill to guard the entrance, and the holes in the window jambs originally secured protective iron grilles. No doubt the rubble walls would have been harled, as at Craigievar.

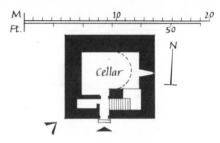

Amisfield Tower, Dumfriesshire (1600). Seen from the south-west.

The ground floor plan is a simple rectangle with a vaulted cellar. A straight stair leads to the first floor.

A typical yett seen from within, hanging against the strong wooden outer door. This iron grating is of peculiar construction.

Dovecot at Balbegno Castle, Kincardineshire.

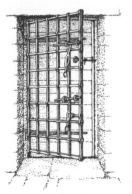

Castle Stewart, Inverness-shire (c. 1625). A mansion house incorporating the features of the tower-house but with the difference of having the towers on the same side of the main block—a modification of the 'Z' type plan—producing a symmetrical design, which was becoming common. In the main the tower-house had ceased to be the fashionable residence of the noble and laird, its place being taken by the mansion house.

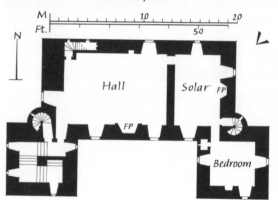

Castle Stewart. First floor plan.

Crathes Castle, Kincardineshire.

It is not uncommon to see a wing in the form of an ordinary house built onto the tower-house, as at Crathes (early 18th century), or separately, nearby, as at Amisfield (17th century), a departure following more peaceful and prosperous times for the laird desiring greater comfort.

Glamis Castle, Angus, is an ancient 'L' plan tower-house where substantial additions in the 17th century produced a mansion, which following the fashion of the time, when viewed from the main drive, attempts to present a symmetrical aspect.

Glamis Castle. First floor plan.

Amisfield Tower.

Dining Room

Lower Hall

N

M | 10 | 20
Ft. | 50

Parish churches

The churches built at this time were generally small and of simple form resembling the medieval kirk and appropriate to the needs of Reformed worship. The building styles were extant Gothic, Netherlandish Renaissance or a mixture of both with elements of the domestic style of the time fashioned in a form peculiar to Scotland by builders largely unknown. Plans were of three types, rectangular, 'T' and cruciform. The first was most common, the second was a peculiarly Scottish manifestation brought about by the addition of a wing or 'aisle' in the middle of the north or south wall built as burial vault with a loft above for the heritor. The third, a development of the second type, was least common, with the pulpit situated in the crossing. In rectangular churches the pulpit was usually placed against the south wall flanked by large windows on either side and in the gables. The entrances, sometimes two, were situated at either end of the south wall. Lofts were commonly built at either end of the church for additional accommodation and have their counterpart in Germany and Scandinavia. Seating consisted of benches or stools and pews. Candles in wooden or metal holders provided illumination. Interiors were colourful though they differed from their medieval counterpart in that decoration was confined to armorial bearings, rolls of guilds, quotations and decorative pattern work and not pictorial representations from the scriptures, the spoken and printed word taking their

Lyne Church (plan).

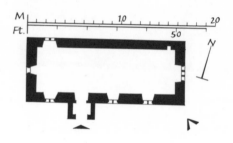

Lyne Church, Peeblesshire (1645), built to a rectangular plan. The exterior rubble walls were originally harled leaving the window dressings exposed. The buttresses on the west end and the porch date from 1886–8, when the church was restored and the belfry was rebuilt. The church contains the original barrel-shaped pulpit and canopied pews, which are now rarely seen in buildings of this period.

place. The bell, being an essential item of parochial equipment, was housed in a belfry over the west gable, which often received special architectural treatment. Towers were less common and very occasionally stood detached. The walls, more usually built of rubble, were invariably harled and whitewashed on the exterior, leaving the dressings of windows and doors exposed.

Two isolated and different churches of this period deserve to be mentioned, Greyfriars (1638), and the Canongate (1688) in Edinburgh, the former on account of its size, a large aisled and arcaded building with a tower, and the latter as a unique example in Britain of a church which recalls a pre-Reformation arrangement, the Latin cross. The south front is a fine example of Netherlandish Renaissance.

Cawdor Church, Nairnshire, built to a 'T' plan. The south aisle and tower were built in 1619, and the belfry stage in the 18th century.

Montgomery Monument, Skelmorlie aisle, Ayrshire, (1636). Built by Sir Robert Montgomery of Skelmorlie. A fine example of an early Renaissance monument under a painted timber barrel-vault.

A drawing showing the arrangement of a post-Reformation church with the fabric cut open. The north aisle, shown here in outline, makes this a 'T' plan church.

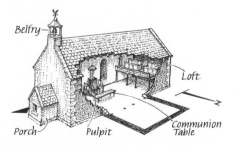

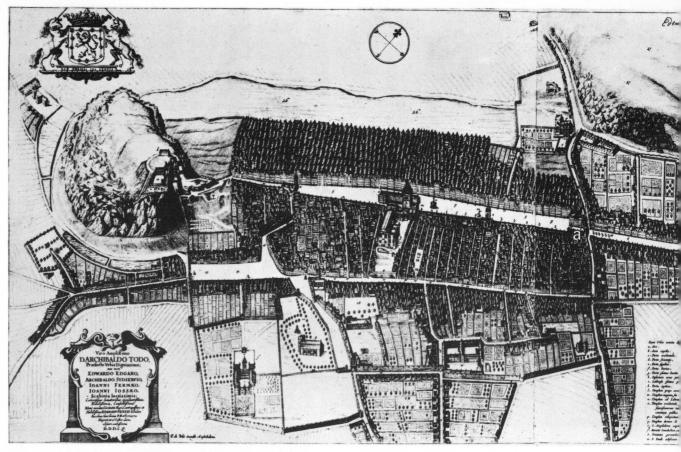

The main features of a walled medieval town are well illustrated in this print of Edinburgh of c. 1647 by the Rev. James Gordon of Rothiemay. The broad High Street and Canongate form together the main thoroughfare along which the principal buildings are situated. By this time, however, Edinburgh was already expanding to the south.

Burgh architecture

During the 17th century, due largely to the development of trade with the continent, there was an increase in the number of burghs. These were in the main at or near navigable waters and were dotted over the east coast from Berwickshire to the Moray Firth and in the west on the Firths of Clyde and Solway. (In the Highlands there were no towns and few real villages.) The layout of these burghs followed the medieval pattern and depended on whether they were situated round a harbour or were inland on some principal trade route. The principal buildings—such as the Tolbooth, the houses of the wealthy merchants, and the town houses of neighbouring lairds—were situated in the High Street or Hie Gait. This was the main thoroughfare and market place, consequently it was broad. Wynds, vennels and closes led off the High Street and here you would find the kirk, the school, the mill and the craftsman. They are usually so named—Kirk Wynd, Mill Wynd... The town was surrounded by the garden or yard walls, which were of uniform height, and backed on to the common land or burgh muir. Entry was by the town gate or port, e.g., West Port, St. Andrews; Netherbow Port, Edinburgh (demolished).

The Netherbow Port, Edinburgh, late 16th and 17th century, was one of the principal gates into the city— marked (a) on large print on the left. (From an old print by John Runciman made shortly before the building was demolished in 1764.)

West Port, St. Andrews, (1589) (renovated in 1843 when the arches over the pavements were built). Looking into the town.

The Tolbooth or Town Hall was generally the most conspicuous building because of its tower, which housed the town bell. The origin of the name explains itself as it was at the tolbooth that taxes and tolls were collected. It served as a court room and council chamber and prison for debtors, and was entered by a forestair, an arrangement commonly seen in the Low Countries.

The houses of the burghs, whether they were large or small, shared a common style. They were built of local rubble, harled and colourwashed. The roofs were steeply pitched and covered with thatch, slate, stone or pantiles, the last most commonly on the east coast, imported as ballast from the Low Countries. The gable ends were generally built in the characteristic crow-steps. Windows were generally small in relation to the wall area. The upper half was glazed while the lower half consisted of openable wooden shutters for ventilation. These were later replaced by casement windows. Dormer windows with carved pediments and finials are common.

Town House, Culross, Fife (1626), the tower was built in 1783.

Lamb's House, Leith.

This drawing illustrates some typical features of Scottish vernacular architecture, such as the pedimented dormer window, the pantiled roof and the crow-stepped gable.

84

Argyll's Lodging (plan).

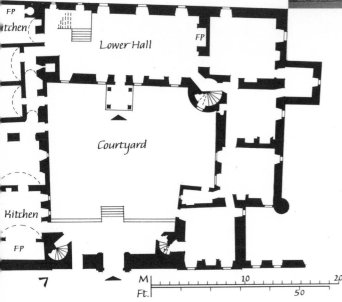

Argyll's Lodging, Stirling, is a splendid example of a town residence of a nobleman. It reached its present form enclosing an irregular quadrangle by a number of additions in the 17th century. The heavily rusticated Renaissance gateway to the street is a good example of the period. (See also page 71.)

Old Hamilton House, Prestonpans, East Lothian (1628), built by an Edinburgh burgess, is of a similar plan but smaller, and more intimate. It represents vernacular architecture of the 'burgh' type at its best. The low street wall is modern, the courtyard originally extended over what is now the street. An unusual feature for this time was the use of the ground floor for living accommodation instead of storage. This did not become general until the 18th century.

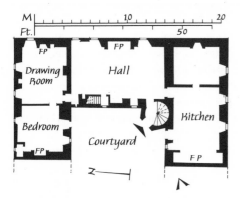

Old Hamilton House (plan).

Culross Palace, Fife: decorated woodwork in the north lodging.

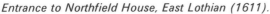

Entrance to Northfield House, East Lothian (1611).

The interior furnishings of the houses of the wealthy merchants could, through their owners' trade connections, outdo in splendour those of the local laird or baron. Painted decoration on plaster and wood, moulded plaster ceilings, rich wall hangings and stoutly-made furniture of local and imported manufacture could grace the rooms sombrely lit with candles in brass candlesticks from Sweden. But usually furnishings were simple.

The dressed stone framing the entrance was occasionally enriched with a simple moulding but more often left plain. The lintel frequently displays the carved initials of the owner and the date of building. Doors were simple and strong, made of vertical planks of wood, nailed to horizontal planks without a frame and hung on iron hinges, fitted with an iron latch and tirling pin and a large iron lock in a wooden case.

Gladstone's Land, Edinburgh (headquarters of The Saltire Society). Stone front replaced timber front in 1631.

In the larger houses the principal rooms were situated on the first floor, and often entered by a forestair. Access to the upper floors was by a newel stair off the stair head or from one of the rooms. Gladstone's Land, Edinburgh, the house of a merchant and burgess, illustrates this. In addition it displays another feature of burgh architecture, the arcaded street front, also to be seen at Duff O'Bracco's House, Elgin, and at houses in Linlithgow. This was a development from the medieval overhanging timber galleries which were either corbelled out or stood on wooden posts. When the owners rebuilt their fronts with stone they had to preserve a passageway.

Duff O'Bracco's House, Elgin (1694).

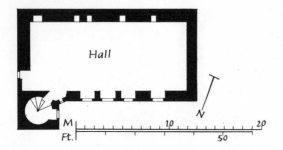

Tailor's Hall, Edinburgh (1621), plan of the first floor. This is one of the very few buildings left which have a connection with the medieval trade-corporations. It now forms part of a large brewery in the heart of the old city. It consists of a rectangular building of originally three stories with a projecting stair tower and entrance in the re-entrant angle, making an 'L' plan, typical of the period.

A peculiar feature of Edinburgh, noted by travellers of the time and still very much part of the scene to-day, is the large number of tall flatted tenements, called 'Lands'. In a walled city whose main street descends from the castle to the palace along a ridge there was no alternative but to build up; nine and ten stories were not uncommon but unknown elsewhere.

A feature seen in the High Street of every burgh was the mercat cross, a symbol of municipal authority. Many of these survive in their original position. They consist of a stone shaft raised on a platform of steps and surmounted by an armorial device, a unicorn or other design. Sometimes the shaft was mounted on a platform and reached by a flight of stairs, this was more common in the wealthier burghs. Proclamations were made at the cross and the market and fair took place around it. At Fettercairn in Kincardineshire (1670), an ell, the standard Scots measure (just over a yard long) is carved on one side of the shaft. No doubt this would settle any disputes of short measure!

The Mercat Cross, Prestonpans, East Lothian (early 17th century), standing in its original position. Others like this at Edinburgh, Perth, Dundee and Aberdeen have been rebuilt and in some cases moved to another site or destroyed.

10   Eighteenth Century

William III (1689–1702); Anne (1702–14); George I (1714–27); George II (1727–60); George III (1760–1820).

Scotland's serious economic depression, England's concern that there should be a Protestant succession to the throne, and her desire for military security on her northern border, were some of the dominant factors which led to the Union of Parliaments in 1707. The Treaty of Union united the two kingdoms under the title of Great Britain. Scotland preserved her own Church and judiciary and was to benefit from commercial equality with England but lost her own parliament.

The Protestant state was firmly established in the 18th century. Though religion tended to play a less important part in the affairs of the country, there continued an active interest in religious matters. The Episcopalian Church which had received severe setbacks following the Jacobite rebellions was not without influence, but Roman Catholicism was still proscribed by law and its political influence was practically non-existent.

After the first quarter of the century, steady and increasing economic progress was made. Commerce, particularly Glasgow's trade with the American colonies, increased rapidly, which in turn stimulated industry. During the latter half of the 18th century industrial progress made rapid strides with textile mills, coal mines, foundries, engineering and shipbuilding. This marked the beginning of the industrial age, though such activity was confined mainly to the central lowland belt, and it is here that we find many of the earliest examples of industrial architecture in Scotland. Wealth accumulated from commerce was available for encouraging home industries.

Attracted by the security of employment which industry offered, an increasing number of people moved from the landward areas to the new industrial areas. Medieval towns like Edinburgh and Glasgow became congested and had to build beyond their old boundaries and fashionable suburbs were built for the well-to-do. Some new towns were begun, like Grangemouth, and Letham in Forfarshire, and others were revived by the stimulus of industrial activity. Social and commercial intercourse between Scotland and England affected the Scots in their choice of furnishings and the design of their houses as well as in matters of dress and social habits. While shipping continued to serve the greater part of the country, canals were built to serve the emergent industrial areas

and new roads were built or old ones improved, with toll-gates to pay for the cost of upkeep and construction. The need for faster transport encouraged the building of lighter and speedier vehicles. This was at a time when half the working population of Scotland was still engaged in agriculture, which at the beginning of the century was primitive and unproductive but began to improve. Enterprising landlords made better use of their land and gave tenants long leases to encourage them to do the same. The benefits of the better methods, however, only gradually covered the country.

In the north, General Wade opened up the Highlands between 1726 and 1733 with a series of roads and bridges, mainly for military purposes, but these also contributed to social progress. Apart from some increase in cattle, the main exportable commodity, agriculture remained backward because of the poor nature of the soil. The seaweed industry brought some benefit, but the introduction of sheep farming was a mixed blessing as it saw the beginning of the Highland Clearances, through which hundreds of families were dispossessed. Many of them made their way to the industrial towns while others went overseas to the new colonies to start life afresh.

The increase of prosperity in the country also brought an increase in the population. Estimated to have been just over a million at the beginning of the century, it had increased by about half by 1800. Many men of note flourished in the latter half of the 18th century—in scholarship, literature, art and medicine—and the principal seats of learning had won high reputations outside Scotland. In addition, the universities expanded and underwent sweeping reforms. There was slow but steady improvement in schools, including the beginning of the establishment of schools in the Highlands and Islands.

Building activity

Until the middle of the century there was little building, though what was built was of great interest. The appearance of the formal country house and the 'Laird's House' is an expression of the more peaceful conditions.

From the middle of the century the upsurge in prosperity encouraged new building of every kind—domestic, civic, ecclesiastical and industrial. The expansion of old towns beyond their walled limits began in Aberdeen, Edinburgh, Glasgow and Perth, e.g., the New Town of

Edinburgh. In the country enterprising landowners began to establish new villages and towns to stimulate trade and industry and to settle farming communities upset by land improvements, e.g., Newcastleton, Roxburghshire. The new formal layout contrasts with the random growth of medieval towns. The 'hall-church' and the 'improved' farmhouse were introduced during this time.

The native building tradition in dressed stone, or rubble and harl, became universal. Houses were roofed with slate, pantile or lead. Timber building and thatch were discouraged, though timber was extensively used structurally, hidden in masonry work. The use of finely dressed stone, called polished ashlar, for Classical façades increased.

Architectural character

The Classical style, introduced to Scotland by William Bruce, was the accepted style for major building. It derived its main inspiration from the English Classicism of Inigo Jones and Christopher Wren, and was by the 1750s fully in step with contemporary trends of British architecture.

Classical design was as much the outcome of the personal taste of the patron as the individual interpretation and skill of the architect. Both patron and designer were travelled and knowledgeable about the latest fashions in architectural design, which they acquired at first hand (for instance on the Grand Tour) and through publications.

The term 'Georgian' is widely used for all the architecture in Britain of this century and the next until about the 1830s. The main exponents in Scotland in the first half of the century were James Smith (d. 1731), and William Adam of Kirkcaldy (1689–1748). William Adam was the last great Scots architect whose style retained traces of native character, but the rapid change of fashion and his admiration for the work of some of his contemporaries (e.g. James Gibbs and Sir John Vanburgh) resulted in his making a more studied approach to the Classical style. His three sons, John (1721–92), Robert (1728–92) and James (1732–94), became famous architects in Britain and introduced the 'Adam' style of design and decoration which made a major contribution to architecture. A number of other Scots architects like Colen Campbell (d. 1729), James Gibbs (1682–1754) and Sir William Chambers (1723–96), worked mainly in England and established international reputations for themselves, but left little work in Scotland.

From about 1750 the Classical style received a fresh impetus from antiquarian study, to which men like the Adam brothers, Gibbs and Chambers contributed significantly. We distinguish the works of this period by the term 'Neo-Classical'. At about the same time there appeared in Britain a new and romantic interest in medieval architecture, in contrast to the severe formalism of the Classical style. This was the beginning of the 'Romantic' movement in architecture.

Characteristic of architecture of this period was symmetry in plans and elevations. The principal floor was at entrance level. Larger windows, which featured from the end of the 17th century, were now common; these were mainly square or round headed, usually of the sash kind, and divided by wooden astragals into small panes. In large houses, roofs were generally 'hipped', without gables, and the wall-head emphasised with a cornice or balustrade. Flat, lead-covered roofs were also built. Classical designs incorporated mature Renaissance motifs (Duff House) or new interpretations from antique originals (University of Edinburgh), while medieval designs were romantically conceived with motifs from castellated and ecclesiastical architecture (Inveraray).

The tradition of the mason and wright survived for the best part of the century to provide some continuity, particularly in the landward areas, where vernacular mannerisms continued longest.

Buildings to see

Classical houses

Haddo House, near Methlick, Aberdeenshire (1732). William Adam. **Duff House,** Banffshire (1730–40). William Adam. **Hopetoun House,** West Lothian (1723–54). William, Robert and John Adam. **Pollok House,** Glasgow (1748 and later). William and John Adam. **Dun House,** Montrose, Angus (c. 1733). William Adam. **Duddingston House,** Edinburgh (1768). Sir William Chambers. **Royal Bank of Scotland** (originally the town house of Sir Laurence Dundas), St. Andrew Square, Edinburgh (1774). Sir William Chambers. **Hawkhill House,** Edinburgh (1757). John Adam. **Moffat House,** Moffat, Dumfriesshire (1762), John Adam. **Cally House,** Kirkcudbrightshire (1765). Robert Mylne. **Preston Hall,** Midlothian. (1790s). Robert Mitchell. **Melville House,** Ladybank, Fife (1701), James Smith (?). **Yester House,** Gifford, East Lothian (c. 1715). James Smith and William and Robert Adam.

Georgian 'Gothic' houses

Inveraray Castle, Argyll (1745–61). Roger Morris. **Culzean Castle,** Ayrshire (1771–92) (N.T.S.). Robert Adam. **Mellerstain,** Gordon, Berwickshire (1770s). Robert Adam. **Pitfour Castle,** Glencarse, Perthshire (1784). Robert Adam. **Braid House,** Hermitage of Braid. Edinburgh (c. 1785). Robert Burn. **Melville Castle,** Dalkeith, Midlothian (1786). James Playfair.

Churches

St. Andrew's, Dundee, Angus (1772). James Craig and Samuel Bell. **Catrine,** Ayrshire (1792). **Lanark Old**

Kirk, Lanark (1774). **St. Andrew's,** Edinburgh (1785). Major Andrew Frazer. Steeple (1789). William Sibbald. **St. Andrew's Parish Church,** Glasgow (1756). Allan Dreghorn. **Inverarity,** Angus (1754). **St. Mungo's,** Penicuik, Midlothian (1771). **Carrington,** Midlothian (1710). **Yester,** near Gifford, East Lothian (1710). **Auldearn,** Nairnshire (1757). **Bellie Parish Kirk,** Fochabers, Morayshire (1798). John Baxter. **St. Nicholas West,** Aberdeen (1755). James Gibbs. **Inveraray,** Argyll (1794). Robert Mylne. **Reay,** Caithness (1739). **Alves,** Morayshire (1769). **Farr,** Sutherland (1774). **St. Ninians Tower,** Stirling (1734).

Civic architecture

Town House, Stirling (1702). Sir William Bruce. **The Midsteeple,** Dumfries (c. 1707). Tobias Bauchop. **Town House,** Sanquhar, Dumfriesshire. **Kintore Town House,** Kintore, Aberdeenshire (1737–47). **Town House,** Haddington, East Lothian (1748). William Adam. Steeple (1831). Gillespie Graham. **Tolbooth,** West Wemyss, Fife (early 18th c.). **Town House,** Dunbar, East Lothian. **Trades House,** Glasgow (1794). Robert Adam. **General Register House,** Edinburgh (1774–1822). Robert and James Adam, completed by Robert Reid. **University of Edinburgh** (1789–1828). Robert Adam, completed by William H. Playfair. **The**

City Chambers (originally the **Royal Exchange),** Edinburgh (1753 and later). John and Robert Adam. **The Exchange Building,** Leith (1788).

Town planning

Edinburgh New Town (started 1767). James Craig. **Inveraray,** Argyll (started in the 1750s). Robert Mylne and John Adam. **Grantown-on-Spey,** Morayshire (c. 1765). **Tomintoul,** Banffshire (1775). **Newcastleton,** Roxburghshire (1793). **Ullapool,** Ross and Cromarty (1788). **Tobermory,** Mull, Argyll (1788). **Gifford,** East Lothian.

Further reading

DUNBAR, JOHN G. *The Historic Architecture of Scotland* London, Batsford 1966

FLEMING, JOHN *Robert Adam and His Circle* London, John Murray 1962

HAY, GEORGE *The Architecture of Scottish Post-Reformation Churches 1560–1843* Oxford, Clarendon Press 1957

SUMMERSON, JOHN *The Architecture in Britain 1530–1830* London, Penguin Books 1953

YOUNGSON, A. J. *The Making of Classical Edinburgh 1750–1840* Edinburgh, University Press 1966

Robert Adam (1728–92).

The Georgian period

Classical Georgian houses

From the beginning of the 18th century a more formal kind of house was built in Scotland both in town and country. This distinguishes itself by having a symmetrical plan and a façade in which windows were regularly placed about a central entrance. These essentials are seen in large and small houses alike and owe their origin to the Renaissance.

With the introduction of Renaissance design came the professional designer, hence most large 18th century buildings are associated with the name of an architect. Architecture in the 18th century, however, was not an exclusive profession as it is to-day; an educated man could design his own house with a mason or architect to advise him. Small houses continued to be built by local craftsmen though now increasingly their designs were taken from the numerous pattern books which were

Hopetoun House, West Lothian (1723–54). William, Robert and John Adam. The east front.

Hopetoun House from the air.

Duff House, Banffshire (1730–40). William Adam.

becoming available.

The careful attention devoted to external appearances was a particular feature of the planning of the large country mansion which was often in a spaciously land-scaped setting, as at Hopetoun House, West Lothian. In the first half of the century such large mansions were rare, as most landed proprietors continued to live in their old houses from preference or necessity. Some, on the other hand, as we saw in the 17th century, improved their accommodation by Georgian style additions.

The dramatic quality of the entrance façade of Duff House results from the combination of the rich Classical treatment of the lower, main storeys, with the 'baronial' character of the skyline and projecting corners. This is a very fine though rare example of the more exuberant work of William Adam, and of Scottish Classical architecture of the first part of the century.

Hopetoun House, begun at the turn of the century by Sir William Bruce, was altered by William Adam and completed by his sons John and Robert in 1754. It displays in the design of its eastern front a more sophisticated type of design. The unified appearance of the main block owes much to the open balustrade which hides the roof line.

Duff House, Banffshire (plan).

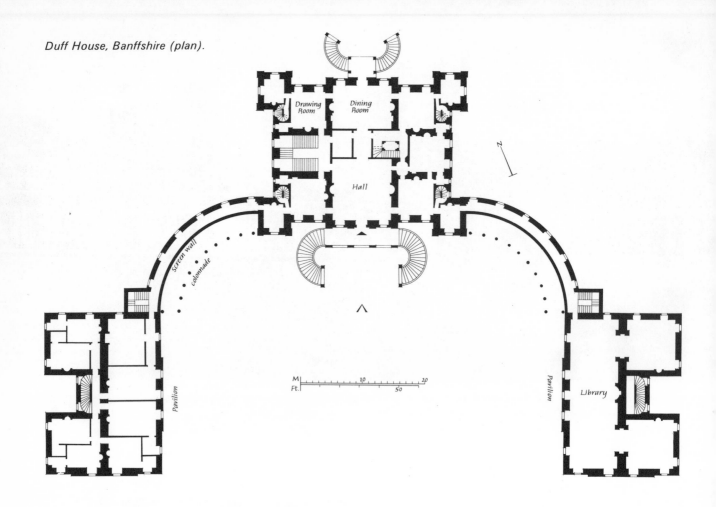

Arniston, Midlothian (1730). The hall decorated by William Adam. Typical of William Adam's interior decoration is the bold use of Classical motifs such as the pediments and 'keystones' over the doors and arches, and the swags and festoons of flowers, foliage and fruits.

The plan of the main block of Duff House illustrates the compact, symmetrical Renaissance arrangement in which the main entrance and hall occupies the centre, with rooms leading off. The projected semi-circular colonnades and screen walls on either side of the main block would have connected with a library and an additional suite of rooms.

At Hopetoun House the pavilions terminating at the wings contain a ballroom and stables, whose use is not betrayed by their external appearance but which rather add up to a very imposing design.

Georgian 'Gothic' houses

The study of the architecture of ancient Greece and Rome which the Renaissance had stimulated, extended by mid-century to the study of medieval art. This is seen in the shape of Gothic forms from ecclesiastical and castellated architecture applied to buildings with elevations and plans of regular symmetrical design. The term 'Romantic Medieval' is given to this seemingly extravagant style which was widely fashionable in Britain. The fanciful recreations of medieval ruins, or 'follies', and 'Gothic' summer houses in large estates are other examples of this trend.

Inveraray Castle, Argyll (1745–61). Roger Morris. This is one of the earliest Georgian houses in Scotland to show the new fashion for Gothic 'dress'. (The conical roofs on the corner towers are later additions.)

Culzean Castle, Ayrshire (1772–92). Robert Adam. Culzean, built during the last quarter of the 18th century, shows castellated features which were characteristic of an aspect of the designs of Robert Adam and the outcome of his studies in Italy. The rooms are elegantly decorated in the distinctive style for which the Adam brothers were famed.

Smaller houses

Characterful houses, less imposing than either Duff or Hopetoun, were built at this time. These also made a feature of the entrance by advancing the centre and crowning it with a classical pediment. The roof could be hipped and the chimneys rose from the inner walls. When the exterior walls were harled, with door and window surrounds and quoins (angles of the building) left exposed, the result was more traditional.

A modest-looking house of symmetrical design began to be built from the beginning of the century. This retained something of the vernacular character and has been called the 'laird's house', because it was built by the small landowner. It became widely adopted for the parish minister, the merchant and the master craftsman, and was the basis of the new 'improved' farmhouse later in the century.

It consisted of a plain rectangular gable-roofed structure of two storeys with an attic. It was usually built of stone and lime and roofed with slate, stone or pantile, or occasionally with thatch. Within, a central staircase led from a small vestibule to the upper floor. The main rooms extended from the front to the back of the house; the kitchen and the parlour were on the ground floor and the bedrooms on the upper floor.

Plans (ground and first floor) of a 'laird's house'— Old Auchentroig, Stirlingshire (1702).

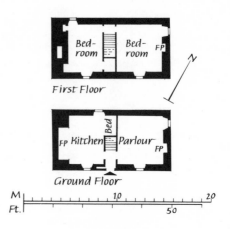

Airds House, Argyll (1738).

In larger houses, the simple plan of the 'laird's house' was extended with dividing walls and corridors and the addition of a service basement, partly below ground level.

House in Front Street, Inveraray, Argyll (1760).

Key House, Falkland, Fife (1713).

The Weaver's Cottage, Kilbarchan, has the traditional character of a rural dwelling, with its flag-stone floor, lime-washed stone walls and low ceiling. This type of building was unaffected by the prevailing fashion.

The Weaver's Cottage, Kilbarchan, Renfrewshire (1723). Exterior and interior.

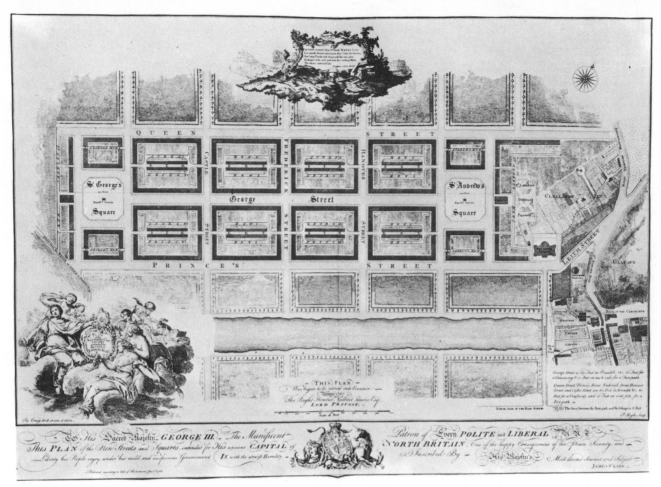

James Craig's plan for the New Town of Edinburgh (1767). (St. George's Square was renamed Charlotte Square.)

Civic architecture and town planning

The expansion of old towns in the second half of the century saw new architectural developments both in street planning and building which owe their origin to the Renaissance.

The New Town of Edinburgh is the most impressive and widely admired of these in Scotland and bears comparison with similar planned schemes of this time elsewhere. The successful design in a competition promoted by the Town Council was by James Craig (1740—95). This was conceived as a symmetrical layout upon a main axis, George Street, terminating in a square at each end; parallel, on the north and south, run two similarly broad streets, connected at right angles along their lengths. Behind the houses facing the main streets, and parallel to them, are narrow lanes which lead to the tradesmen's houses and mews. This orderly arrangement was successfully added to in the early decades of the 19th century.

Charlotte Square (north side), Edinburgh (1791). Robert Adam.

Late 18th century houses in Edinburgh (57—61 North Castle Street). This block consists of two main-door houses with basements. Above these are flats served from the street by a common entrance (centre door) and stairway. A traditional arrangement of town houses in Scotland.

Houses of the first new town developments were of varying heights, gable-roofed and adjoining one another.

One of the earliest designs in Scotland of a unified street frontage was made by Robert Adam for Charlotte Square, Edinburgh, in 1791 (above). It consists of a number of self-contained houses of three main floors, as one architectural unit, like a mansion. This was followed in the subsequent development of the New Town of Edinburgh and elsewhere, though flatted or tenemented dwellings are more usual.

The noble design of this frontage is typical of the work of Robert Adam, in which the Classical motifs from Roman architecture have been interpreted with great refinement. The channel-jointed stone work at entrance level contrasts with the polished ashlar of the upper storeys; semi-circular arches, Venetian windows (over the middle entrance), carved festoons and roundels are some of the recurring features in Robert Adam's designs. (No 5 is the headquarters of the National Trust for Scotland.)

The graciously designed interiors of these houses are sensitively ornamented with plasterwork in the characteristic Adam style. The Adam brothers were also noted for their distinguished design of fireplaces and furniture.

Even when not on such a grand scale, the design of Georgian housing was impressive because of its harmony.

The approach to new village planning in the 18th and early 19th century followed the same principles of a grid-like layout incorporating a broad central main street. These can be seen in Fochabers and Grantown-on-Spey, Morayshire; Inveraray, Argyll; and Newcastleton, Roxburghshire. They make interesting comparisons with medieval towns.

Inveraray is an early and important example of town planning on a small scale and was built by the local landowner. The original street plan was designed by John Adam and Robert Mylne, the latter of whom also designed the church. Like other planned towns and villages of this time, the church was often situated at a focal point in the layout of the streets. (Regrettably the steeple was removed during the last war, but efforts are being made to have it restored.)

In most civic building Classical design showed itself chiefly in the regularity of the frontages and in the larger size of windows, with vernacular mannerisms still very much in evidence. The Town Hall was often distinguished by the addition of a tower rising from the roof and the forestairs could be curved.

When the services of an architect were obtained buildings were designed in a more thorough-going Classicism. This was notably so in the larger burghs such as Aberdeen, Dundee, Edinburgh, Glasgow, all of which still possess a number of fine buildings by well known architects. Edinburgh is fortunate in having many, most of which date from the end of the 18th century or the beginning of the 19th

Late 18th century tenemented dwelling-houses of work people at Inveraray, Argyll, built of harled rubble with slate roofs. Entrance is by a common passage. These houses effectively combine the essence of Georgian design and vernacular tradition, and were tastefully restored between 1958—60 by Ian G. Lindsay, architect.

Town House, Kintore, Aberdeenshire (1737 and 1747).

University of Edinburgh (1789–1828). From Robert Adam's original design for the east front. The east front of the present building and the west side of the quadrangle (or great court) were carried out mainly to the original design. The rest is a redesigned adaptation by William H. Playfair, who completed the work in 1828. The dome was designed by Sir R. Rowand Anderson in 1887.

The New College, University of Edinburgh (plan).
  The original layout consisted of a compact symmetrical arrangement enclosing two courtyards. Entrance was through a portico (see above), which was flanked by professors' houses, and an atrium or forecourt, from which arcaded passages led to the main courtyard. In the redesigning the atrium was omitted and the professors' houses were replaced by lecture rooms.

Maths

Great Hall

Anat

Humanity

Great Court

Phy

Museum

Natural History

Chemis

History

First Court

Professors'

Houses

M   10   20
Ft.   50

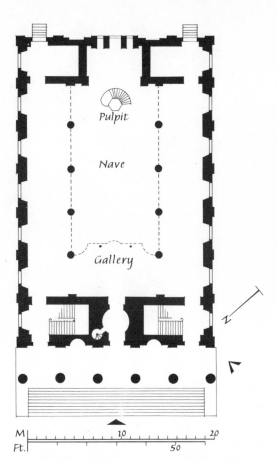

St. Andrew's Parish Church, Glasgow (plan).

Churches

In the 18th century, town churches showed a marked change, with Classical design predominating. These now often included a steeple rising from the roof and a Classical portico to dignify the entrance. From mid-century there began a change both inside and outside. In the internal arrangement galleries were built along both long walls and across one end and the pulpit was placed near the centre of the opposite end. This introduces a new type known as the 'hall-church' and derives from the designs of Christopher Wren and James Gibbs.

Country churches remained on the whole more traditional and varied little in plan from the previous century. The most notable difference was in the increased size of the windows, now often round-headed and built with light wooden glazing bars and plain glass. This and the introduction of Classical design in the belfry or tower were the main acknowledgements to the prevailing architectural fashion. The pulpit stood against the middle of one long wall, usually the southern one, and lofts or galleries were built across the end walls.

St. Andrew's Parish Church, Glasgow (1756). Allan Dreghorn. Viewed from the west.

Auldearn, Nairnshire (1757).

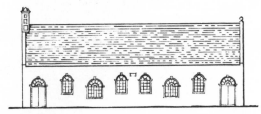

103

Kilravock Bridge (the White Bridge) near Cawdor, Nairnshire.

Bridges

From the beginning of the century there was an improvement in bridge design, with wider carriageways and longer spans. The increasing use of wheeled transport, and road building, helped to open up the country and contributed to its prosperity. The 'Wade' bridges were of the simplest construction with one or more semi-circular arches spanning the river over which ran a road wide enough to take a carriage. Most of our humpbacked bridges date from this time.

Where the road served as an approach to an estate the owner sometimes employed an architect to supply the design for the new bridge, which could then have a more distinguished appearance.

Shira Bridge, near Inveraray, Argyll (1775). Robert Mylne.

11 Nineteenth Century

George III (1760–1820); George IV (1820–30); William IV (1830–37); Queen Victoria (1837–1901).

In the main the history of Scotland in the 19th century is inseparably bound up with the history of the United Kingdom. Economic expansion brought about by the industrial revolution, and events abroad such as the French Revolution, the American Civil War, the progress of the empire and the fluctuations of world trade influenced political and social developments in Scotland in much the same way as they did in England. Nevertheless Scotland did not lose her national identity. She retained her old judiciary and Church and much of her educational system, and developed something of a national spirit in politics which tended towards liberalism and made a significant contribution in the Parliament at Westminster.

The rapid developments of the time in political and social fields also had their effect upon the Church. While Scotland remained staunchly Presbyterian, differences of opinion brought about divisions and unions within the Church and were responsible for a major split in 1843 when the Free Church broke away from the main body and formed an important influential group in the spiritual and social life of the nation. This brought about an increase in church building. The emancipation of Roman Catholics reflects the greater tolerance of the time. The considerable increase in their numbers was mainly due to the influx of Irish immigrants.

During the 19th century, Scotland moved from being primarily an agricultural nation to being mainly industrialised. Natural resources contributed to this change. In the central lowland belt there were rich deposits of coal and iron ore. Good estuaries provided harbours for importing raw materials, and for exporting. Consequently this became the area of the greatest population increase and prosperity.

Building peculiar to industry and commerce made its appearance over the country in the shape of factories, mills, warehouses, railway stations, bridges and harbour installations.

Communications were extended and developed to meet the needs of industrial expansion. The sailing ship was being replaced before the close of the century by the steam-ship. The railways, used in a limited way at first, came into general use in the 1840s and took over from the canals and roads as the main form of industrial transport. Roads were greatly extended, and from about mid-century horse-drawn buses and tramcars provided transport in the larger cities. This contributed significantly to suburban development.

Efficient agriculture in the lowlands took advantage of the general prosperity and this is reflected in the 'improved' farmhouse, which was being built more extensively from about this time. In the Highlands, however, apart from cattle-raising, fishing and the sea-weed industry, there were no natural assets to bring prosperity. Here poverty and overpopulation were aggravated by insufficient cultivable land. The Highland Clearances forced many Highlanders to move to the areas of industrial development or to emigrate to the colonies.

The rapid industrial expansion created appalling social problems among a large proportion of the working people, especially in conditions of employment, housing and health. Robert Owen's efforts to provide good living and working conditions at New Lanark were exceptional. The population increased enormously in the industrial areas and there was much overcrowding in the centres of old towns where housing had fallen into neglect and become slums. Early areas of industrial housing which, while accommodating people near their work, lacked proper sanitation and social amenities, became the black spots of the future. Successive governments passed legislation to bring about better conditions and so made a beginning to the social services. The relief of the poor, conditions of work, local government, education, public health and housing were becoming matters of national concern.

In the fields of learning and the arts, the period produced many men and women of note. While Scotsmen were prominent in many activities in Britain, many also made their names abroad as ambassadors, administrators, missionaries, soldiers, doctors, engineers and in the arts.

Building activity

Except during times of national unrest caused by war or depression, building activity increased steadily during the first half of the century. In the second half there was a more rapid increase of building of every kind, far exceeding that of any previous time. The extent of this can be seen widely over the country, but more particularly in the lowlands.

New developments in transport, besides making

available to a wider market the building resources of a quarry or brickworks, also encouraged new suburban development.

Building methods and materials were in the main traditional. Stone was used for walls, timber for floors, roofs and structural parts, and slate for roofing. Brick was beginning to be used more widely. Iron was used only in a limited way at first (e.g. to support galleries in churches) and usually cast with architectural decoration to harmonise with its setting. Its use on a more extensive scale in architecture was rare, e.g. Gardner's ('The Iron Building') in Glasgow and the Royal Scottish Museum, Edinburgh. Large plant houses provide another example.

In structures of an engineering character such as bridges, viaducts, railway stations and factories, traditional materials as well as new materials—iron, steel and plate glass—were used. In factories and warehouses particularly, the advantage in the use of an iron framework in combination with brick was in its fireproof qualities.

Architectural character

The Romantic Movement of the end of the 18th century which had seen the revival of the Classical and Medieval styles continued into the first part of the 19th century, the Late Georgian period, but with a difference. The original Greek and Roman models were now more closely studied and re-created, and the revival of medieval architecture received a fresh impetus from the writers and architects of the time. These included Sir Walter Scott, with his Romantic novels, and Augustus W. N. Pugin, the English architect, who wrote analytical and descriptive works on the Gothic period. Architects for the first time were given a true guide to the principles of medieval architecture, in much the same way that Robert Adam and others had given a guide to Classical architecture in the 18th century.

In the Victorian age architecture departed from the formal rules of the Georgian period and became predominantly the expression of individual architects. (The beginning of this change was already apparent in the second half of the 18th century.) The main reason for this break with the past was the emergence of the new industrial society and the variety of its building needs. Architecture reflects the new freedom which results from this change. The increasing popularity of architectural and archaeological publications, and travel, widened the field of knowledge in these matters and helped towards a revival of all historical styles. The best Victorian architecture was an expression of pride and self-confidence and the architects' personal interpretation and skilful adaptation of period styles.

Before the end of the century a new attitude to historical revivalism was forming; this, however, was limited to a small but important group of architects (Webb, Shaw and Voysey), mainly in England, associated with the New Art, or 'Art Nouveau' movement. Its followers concerned themselves with a re-appraisal of design based on sound traditional craftsmanship and confined almost entirely to domestic architecture. One of the leading figures in this movement and an acknowledged pioneer of the modern architecture of the 20th century was Charles Rennie Mackintosh (1868–1928) of Glasgow. At the turn of the century Mackintosh and the Art Nouveau circle in Glasgow made a considerable impression on the continent, though their influence in Scotland was small and their works were almost entirely limited to Glasgow and its environs.

Buildings to see

Neo-Classical style
The Old Royal High School, Edinburgh (1829). Thomas Hamilton. **Royal Scottish Academy,** Edinburgh (1823 and 1836). William H. Playfair. **Surgeons' Hall,** Edinburgh (1832). William H. Playfair. **St. George's Church,** Edinburgh (1814). Robert Reid. **St. Mary's Church,** Edinburgh (1824). Thomas Brown.
Georgian street development, Edinburgh—Heriot Row; Abercrombie Place; Northumberland Street; Drummond Place; London Street; Great King Street—first extensions to the New Town, planned by Robert Reid and William Sibbald (1802–c. 1810).
Georgian street development, Edinburgh—Randolph Crescent; Moray Place; Great Stuart Street; Ainslie Place; Glenfinlas Street; St. Colme Street; Forres Street; Albyn Street; Wemyss Place; Darnaway Street—further extensions to the New Town, planned by James Gillespie Graham (1822).
Georgian street development, Edinburgh—Danube Street; St. Bernard's Crescent; Carlton Street; Dean Terrace—designed by James Milne (1824).
St. Bernard's Church, Edinburgh (1823). James Milne. **Stirling's Library (Royal Exchange),** Glasgow (1830). David Hamilton. **Royal Bank of Scotland,** Royal Exchange Square, Glasgow (1827). Archibald Elliott. **Dollar Academy,** Clackmannanshire (1818). William H. Playfair. **Montrose Academy,** Angus (1815). David Logan. **St. Giles' Church,** Elgin (1828). Archibald Simpson. **Erskine Marykirk,** Stirling (1826). **Ayr Town Hall** (1828). Thomas Hamilton. **Falkirk Town Hall** (1813). David Hamilton.

Romantic Medieval style
Scone Palace, Perth, Perthshire (1803 and earlier). **Abbotsford House,** Melrose, Roxburghshire (1823). Edward Blore and William Atkinson. **St. Andrew's Cathedral,** Glasgow (1816). James Gillespie Graham. **Ceres Church,** Fife (1806). **Newlands Church,** Peeblesshire (1838). **St. Paul's Church,** Perth (1807).

John Paterson. **Glenorchy Church,** Dalmally, Argyll (1811). **Cairndon Church,** Argyll (1816). **St. John's Chapel,** Edinburgh (1818). William Burn. **Kincardine-in-Menteith,** Perthshire (1816). Richard Crichton. **Comries,** Old, Perthshire (1805). John Stewart. **Dunino,** Fife (1826). **The Governor's House,** Old Calton Jail, Edinburgh (1815). Archibald Elliott.

Victorian architecture (c. 1840–1900)
Marischal College, Aberdeen (1836–44). Archibald Simpson. **National Commercial Bank,** Gordon Street, Glasgow (1855). David Rhind. **Lansdowne Church,** Glasgow (1863). John Honeyman. **Bank of Scotland,** St. Vincent Place, Glasgow (1869). John T. Rochead. **Caledonian Road Church,** Glasgow (1857). Alexander Thomson. **Great Western Terrace,** Glasgow (*c.* 1870). Alexander Thomson. **21–39 Hyndland Road,** Glasgow (1874). Alexander Thomson. **Royal Faculty of Procurators,** Glasgow (1854). Charles Wilson. **Christian Science Church,** La Belle Place, Glasgow (1857). Charles Wilson. **Barony North Church,** Glasgow (1878). John Honeyman. **Stock Exchange,** Glasgow (1877). John Burnet. **College of Dramatic Art,** Glasgow (1886). Sir John J. Burnet. **Cornhill House,** Glasgow (1881). James Sellars. **Sun Life Building** (former), West George Street and Renfield Street, Glasgow (1893). William Leiper.
Donaldson's Hospital, Edinburgh (1851). William H. Playfair. **National Gallery of Scotland,** Edinburgh (1857). William H. Playfair. **New College,** Edinburgh (1846). William H. Playfair. **Assembly Hall,** Edinburgh (1850). David Bryce. **Tolbooth St. John's Church,** Edinburgh (1844). James Gillespie Graham. **Scottish National Portrait Gallery and Museum of Antiquities,** Edinburgh (1890). Sir R. Rowand Anderson. **McEwan Hall,** Edinburgh (1894). Sir R. Rowand Anderson. **Daniel Stewart's College,** Edinburgh (1853). David Rhind. **Fettes College,** Edinburgh (1870). David Bryce. **Cathedral Church of St. Mary,** Edinburgh (1879). Sir George Gilbert Scott. **Gardner's 'The Iron Building',** Jamaica Street, Glasgow (1856). John Baird and R. McConnell. **Royal Scottish Museum,** Edinburgh (1861). Captain Fowke, Royal Engineers.

Industrial Buildings, Houses and Bridges
New Lanark, Lanarkshire (late 18th and early 19th c.). (mills and village). **Well Court,** (housing and community centre), Dean Village, Edinburgh (1884). Sydney Mitchell. **Baxter's Lower Dens Jute Mills,** Dundee (1866). **Deanston Cotton Mills,** Perthshire (early 19th c.). **Cheapside Bonding Company Warehouse** (originally a mill), Glasgow (1806). **Spey Bridge,** Craigellachie, Banffshire (1815). Thomas Telford. Engineer. **Dean Bridge,** Edinburgh (1831). Thomas Telford.

Engineer. **Tweed Bridge,** Kelso, Roxburghshire (1803). John Rennie. Engineer. **Hutton Suspension Bridge,** Berwickshire (1820). Samuel Brown. Engineer. **Forth Railway Bridge** (1890). Sir John Fowler and Sir Benjamin Baker. Engineers.

Art Nouveau
Glasgow School of Art (1897–9 and 1907–9). Charles Rennie Mackintosh. **'Glasgow Herald' Building** (1895). Charles Rennie Mackintosh. **St. Cuthbert's and Queen's Cross Church,** Glasgow (1899). Charles Rennie Mackintosh.

Further reading
BUTT, JOHN *Industrial Archaeology of Scotland* Newton Abbot, David and Charles 1967
BUTT, JOHN; DONNACHIE, IAN L.; HUME, JOHN R. *Industrial History in Pictures—Scotland* Newton Abbot David and Charles 1968
CROSSLAND, J. BRIAN *Victorian Edinburgh* Letchworth, Wayfair 1966
DUNBAR, JOHN G. *The Historic Architecture of Scotland* London, Batsford 1966
GOMME, ANDOR and WALKER, DAVID *Architecture of Glasgow* London, Lund Humphries 1968
HAY, GEORGE *The Architecture of Scottish Post-Reformation Churches 1560–1843* Oxford, Clarendon Press 1957
MACLEOD, ROBERT *Charles Rennie Mackintosh* London, Country Life 1968
WALKER, D. M. *Architects and Architecture in Dundee, 1770–1914* Abertay Historical Society 1955

Late Georgian architecture

Romantic Medievalism and Neo-Classicism

Romantic Medievalism and Neo-Classicism are characteristic of Late Georgian architecture. Dunninald in Angus is typical of the former. It displays in its plan a preference for an irregular lay-out which was a departure, already noticeable at the end of the last century, from the regular Georgian plan. The fanciful use of castellated features at the wall-head combined with English Late Gothic window treatment has resulted in giving this mansion a picturesque romantic appearance. This fashion was confined mainly to large mansions and ecclesiastical architecture.

Dunninald (plan).

Dunninald, Angus (1832). James Gillespie Graham. Entrance front.

The Old Royal High School, Edinburgh (1829). Thomas Hamilton.

The Old Royal High School, Edinburgh, is a fine example of the Neo-Classical style. It displays in its general mass and careful studied detail the splendour of its ancient architectural origin. This was the outcome of a renewed interest in the antique originals themselves as opposed to the earlier Renaissance interpretation.

St. Bernard's Crescent, Edinburgh (1824). James Milne. This was one of a number of streets speculatively built by Sir Henry Raeburn, the painter, which are typical of the best Late Georgian architecture.

Georgian street development in the 19th century. Edinburgh.

During the early years of the 19th century the New Town of Edinburgh continued to grow in an orderly fashion and assumed its present form by about the end of the first quarter. The top of the aerial photograph shows James Craig's New Town; the lower left is the first addition to this by Robert Reid and William Sibbald between about 1802 and 1810. The lower right is the extensions planned by James Gillespie Graham in *c.* 1822. Similar developments on a fairly grand scale followed, but with the expansion of industry and the railways such good town planning gradually broke down.

Oblong hall-churches with galleries, of the type which appeared in the second half of the 18th century, were the kind now mostly built. These were either in the Georgian 'Gothic' style or the Neo-Classical style. In the larger burghs the Neo-Classical designs often included a temple-like portico to distinguish the entrance at one end, and a tower of Classical proportions rising from the roof, to give a measure of height and dignity to the composition (see page 103).

Though the Episcopal and Roman Catholic churches differed from those of the Church of Scotland in their planning and internal arrangements, they were built in the current architectural styles, but generally favouring the Gothic.

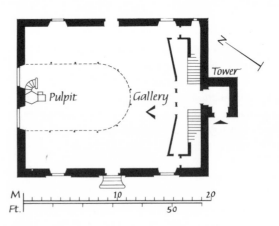

A hall-church at Ceres, Fife (1806), with a 'horse-shoe' gallery (plan).

Interior of Ceres Church, Fife.

110

Donaldson's Hospital (a school), Edinburgh (1851). William H. Playfair. 'Tudor-Gothic' style.

Victorian architecture

Victorian architecture (*c.* 1840–1900) is characterised by contrasting historical styles, both native and imported, and the architect's freedom of interpretation. Commonly the Classical styles were used for public buildings, banks and commercial houses, and the Gothic styles for ecclesiastical architecture. In the design of private houses, on the other hand, all historical styles were freely adapted. The best Victorian architecture displays a high order of academic achievement and originality in meeting the needs of the time.

National Commercial Bank, Gordon Street, Glasgow (1857). David Rhind. In the spirit of the 'Italian High Renaissance'.

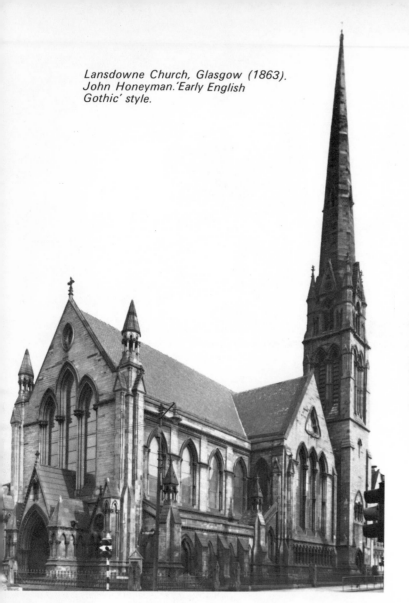

Lansdowne Church, Glasgow (1863). John Honeyman.'Early English Gothic' style.

Tolbooth St. John's Church, Edinburgh (1844). James Gillespie Graham. 'Late Gothic Decorated' style.

21—39 Hyndland Road, Glasgow (1874). Alexander Thomson. 'Neo-Classical' style.

Scottish National Portrait Gallery and Museum of Antiquities, Edinburgh (1890). Sir R. Rowand Anderson. 'Venetian Gothic' style.

Egyptian Halls, Union Street, Glasgow (1871). Alexander Thomson.

Typical of Victorian architecture was the use of plate glass in sash windows, the more extensive use made of polished ashlar, for facing, and bay windows.

Sculptural embellishment on the whole was formal and lacking the vitality characteristic of the original models. This was because masons were no longer working in an inherited tradition but from the paper patterns drawn up by others.

Balmoral Castle, Aberdeenshire (1855). William Smith of Aberdeen.

Overtoun House, Dumbartonshire (1858). James Smith of Glasgow.

Scottish Neo-Baronial

The revival of late castellated and vernacular forms in Scottish architecture was encouraged by the rebuilding of Balmoral Castle in the 1850s. The resulting style was picturesque and sometimes extravagant. A comparison of these examples with Scottish architecture of the 16th and 17th centuries will show the main sources of their designers' inspiration.

Tenements in a residential district, Edinburgh (c. 1880).

A Victorian villa, Edinburgh (c. 1870).

A Victorian tenement in an industrial district (c. 1880). Late Victorian tenements such as these were an advance on what had existed before, as running water and sanitation were included in each house. The accommodation consisted commonly of one or two rooms each with a sleeping recess, and a bathroom.

Good town planning of the late 18th and 19th century broke down after the 1840s with the development of the railways and the rapid unplanned industrial expansion.

The great demand for housing was largely met by the speculative builder, who erected imposing, many-roomed villas and semi-detached houses in the suburbs for the well-to-do, and blocks of tenements and terraces in industrial districts for the artisan.

Industrial architecture and structural engineering

The name 'architect-engineers' is sometimes given to distinguish the men who, working as pioneers in the field of structural engineering, created works of artistic merit. With the new materials at their disposal they solved complex problems in a straightforward manner in building bridges, viaducts, railway stations and harbour installations. These outstanding feats of engineering so characteristic of their time make a strong contrast to the contemporary architecture.

Spey Bridge, Craigellachie, Banffshire (1815). Thomas Telford (engineer). The stone turrets at the bridge abutments are an interesting concession to the taste of the time, though of greater significance is the use of prefabricated cast iron in its construction.

The Dean Bridge, Edinburgh (1831). Thomas Telford. Stone construction. Bridges with level roadways were more usual from the beginning of the century.

The Forth Railway Bridge (1890). Sir John Fowler and Sir Benjamin Baker (engineers). Steel construction on the cantilever principle. The bridge was recognised in its day as an outstanding feat of engineering and is a widely-acclaimed example of the creative genius of that time.

New Lanark, Lanarkshire (late 18th and early 19th century). Cotton mills and village. This was the site of Robert Owen's social experiment for a self-contained industrial community. It was world-famous and became an example for advocates of social and educational reform.

Industrial architecture, a term used to describe building for industry in its widest sense, was usually regarded as the province of the engineer. The purpose of these structures is generally very evident in their design. It was this functional aspect which made a profound appeal to architects of the 20th century who were working out a new architectural expression.

Baxter's Lower Dens jute mills, Dundee (1866). Peter Carmichael (engineer).

Art nouveau

The building at the close of the century which showed a fresh approach to architectural design was, appropriately, an art school. Glasgow School of Art was the first large building the design of which was a departure from the period-styles. Mackintosh in designing this building had returned to the fundamental principles of architecture, and had shown an enlightened respect for the native tradition without imitating it.

Glasgow School of Art (1907–9). The Library. An interior design which is surprisingly modern.

Glasgow School of Art (1897–9 and 1907–9). Charles Rennie Mackintosh.

12   Twentieth Century

Edward VII (1901–10); George V (1910–36); George VI (1936–52); Elizabeth II (1952–   ).

Scotland in the 20th century must be thought of in relation to the whole of Britain and the world in general. The effect of two world wars, the rapid advance of technological and scientific discoveries, the fluctuations of world trade and the policies of different political parties conditioned the lives of the people in Scotland as much as if not more than in the rest of the United Kingdom.

The end of the 19th century and the years before the First War were in the main a period of booming trade. Shipbuilding and the coal industry reached their highest output in 1913. There was great prosperity for a few, and many ordinary people were reasonably well off. But for the majority of the working population, especially those in the industrial lowland belt, there was an acute shortage of housing. Agriculture was depressed and employed fewer workers, though some farming prospered under efficient husbandry and mechanisation.

Road communications improved considerably and there were now motor cars and bicycles, and in towns the motorbus and the electric tramcar replaced horse-drawn public transport. In social welfare, legislation was passed for old age pensions and national insurance, and the Highlands and Islands medical service was started. The school leaving age was raised to fourteen. In Parliament the Scottish Grand Committee was made a permanent committee to ensure that Scottish bills would receive a more sympathetic hearing.

For the duration of the First World War political differences and nationalist sentiments were obscured while an all-out effort towards winning the war controlled people's lives. But the end of the war brought disillusion and discontent. Heavy industry and agriculture languished and unemployment increased. Changes in local government were introduced, affecting education, public health and local services. These replaced earlier parish councils and boards. By the end of the 'twenties the financial problems of the world had become so acute that their repercussions were felt everywhere and resulted in the General Depression of 1931.

Some of the anti-depression measures brought in by the National Government included the modernisation of the fishing industry, subsidies to farmers and import controls. Efforts to induce new industries to settle in the distressed areas resulted in the development of new towns —

Hillington near Glasgow (1937), Carfin, Chapelhall and Larkhall in Lanarkshire (1939). By this time some stability had been achieved and re-armament helped to increase employment.

Some wartime legislation pointed to the future, such as the creation of the North of Scotland Hydro-electric Board, government control of railways and mines, and the publication of the Beveridge Report on National Welfare.

After the Second World War Scotland did not suffer from economic depression because the economy of the United Kingdom was in a healthier state, due to the new consciousness of the need for economic planning. A programme of nationalisation, and of social welfare based on the Beveridge Report, was implemented. The expansion of the medical services and the raising of the school leaving age to fifteen had an effect on building. Government encouragement of fishing and farming, the Forestry Commission, the Hydro-electric Board and the Scottish Tourist Board have helped to increase opportunities and employment in the Highlands.

Under the new Town and Country Planning Acts, new towns are being established and re-development of old towns is encouraged with government assistance. The Scottish Council (Development and Industry) has helped to introduce employment in new manufactories of all kinds.

The industrial scene now includes some of the most modern and sophisticated buildings in the world, such as the nuclear power stations, hydro-electric generating stations, smelting plants, pulp mills, oil refineries and the latest coal-fired generating stations. The transport needs of modern industry have resulted in large new networks of roads, although in town and country alike, there is increasing traffic congestion. This is one of the problems to be solved by modern town-planners.

Building activity

The general prosperity inherited from late Victorian times continued up to the First World War. This is reflected in the large number of commercial and civic buildings, as well as churches and schools, erected in cities and towns throughout the land. Private housing of all kinds also shared in this boom but tended to tail off in the years before the war. Housing for the working classes was so inadequate that it was the subject of a Royal Commission in 1917.

119

After the war the unsettled conditions curtailed building but the Government began to give financial help to local authorities for municipal housing schemes. Private developers were also building and new suburbs were created on the outskirts of most of our towns and cities. This was not sufficient to solve the housing problem, however, and was creating the new problem of unplanned expansion encroaching on the countryside, and 'ribbon development'—building along the existing highways on the outskirts of towns.

After 1929 the reunited Church was faced with a surplus of churches in the older parishes and the need to provide new churches in the developing suburbs.

In the 'thirties and during the last war serious attempts were made to tackle the housing problem. Reports were published dealing with various aspects of housing; design, construction, planning, furnishing and so on. The Saltire Society was formed in 1936 to preserve Scottish traditions and culture and to promote and establish, amongst other things, good standards in housing design and to recognise them by their awards. All this did produce better standards of accommodation but design still lagged behind. Since the last war, however, standards of design have improved.

Expansion in the medical and social services, and new ideas in education and housing are resulting in more building in these fields than ever before. Industrial and commercial buildings have had to be brought up-to-date as modern methods require modern buildings. Not since Victorian times has the demand for new building been on such a scale or resulted in so rapid a change in the appearance of many of our towns and cities. Not only are new buildings being constructed but the best of the old are being refurbished under restoration schemes (see page 129).

To the traditional building materials of timber, stone, slate and tile, there were added in the 19th century iron, steel and plate glass, while bricks, which were commonly used elsewhere, began to be more widely used in Scotland. The 20th century introduced reinforced concrete (see page 127), new alloys (e.g., aluminium and stainless steel) and new synthetic substances for external and internal facing and insulating which help to make it possible to build thinner and lighter walls. Above all, the scientific study of building problems, the introduction of new materials, new ways of using traditional materials and the need to build economically have been important factors in creating the architecture of to-day. There is close co-operation between the architect and the engineers, co-ordinating the various highly specialised branches of building construction.

Architectural character

Up to the First World War, architectural design in Scotland, as elsewhere, had become an academic display in historical styles. But there were signs of a break with the past. In Scotland these are to be seen mainly in Glasgow in the designs of Mackintosh, Salmon (the younger), Gaff Gillespie and others associated with the Art Nouveau style. This departure from accepted standards was short-lived however.

During the inter-war years architects readily accepted the advantages which new materials and methods made available and their designs begin to show this. Externally buildings were plainer in appearance, window openings were larger and decoration was in low relief, sometimes with classical overtones. By this time the revival of historical styles was fairly obviously out of place. A new approach to architectural design was needed, and was forthcoming.

To understand the development of modern architecture one must look back to the 19th century, to the work of the great engineers (Telford, Paxton, Cubitt, Brunel); to the creators of the new English domestic architecture (Shaw, Voysey and others); to the work of Charles Rennie Mackintosh and his circle in Glasgow. All of these made a profound impact on the continent in their time, where, too, new ideas were fermenting. From the beginning of the 20th century the main experiments took place in Germany, Austria, Holland and the United States, culminating in the inter-war years in the first really modern architecture. Serious attempts were made to relate the discoveries of the 19th and 20th centuries to the changed needs of a modern society and resulted in an entirely new form of architectural expression, the full effect of which did not appear in Scotland until after 1950, half a century after the pioneer work of Charles Rennie Mackintosh!

The architect, as the artist, designs his buildings to-day with careful thought for their use, working from the inside outwards, as it were. At the same time he takes full advantage of modern scientific methods and materials. The best architecture of today is that in which the architect has successfully used the new materials and techniques in an imaginative and pleasing way, stimulated by the aesthetic possibilities which are presented to him.

Buildings to see

Art Nouveau (1900–c. 1914)
Windyhill, Kilmacolm, Renfrewshire (1901). Charles Rennie Mackintosh. **Hill House,** Helensburgh, Dumbartonshire (1902). Charles Rennie Mackintosh. **Scotland Street School,** Glasgow (1904). Charles Rennie Mackintosh. **Glasgow School of Art,** Glasgow (completed 1909). Charles Rennie Mackintosh. **Lion Chambers,** Glasgow (1905). James Salmon II and J. Gaff Gillespie.

Academic revivals
St. Peter's R.C. Church, Edinburgh (1908). Sir Robert Lorimer. **University Library,** St. Andrews, Fife (1909). Sir Robert Lorimer. **Marischal College,** Aberdeen (extensions 1906—Façade, Mitchell Hall and upper part of tower). Alexander Marshall Mackenzie. **McGeoch's,** 28 West Campbell Street, Glasgow (1905). Sir J. J. Burnet. **Scottish Provident Institution,** Glasgow (1906). J. M. Dick Peddie. **Corner of Hope Street and West George Street,** Glasgow (1902). John A. Campbell. **The Standard Life Assurance Co.,** George Street, Edinburgh (1901). J. M. Dick Peddie. **St. Margaret's,** Braemar, Aberdeenshire (1904). Sir John Ninian Comper. **'The Scotsman' Offices,** Edinburgh (1904). J. B. Dunn. **Midlothian County Buildings,** Edinburgh (1904). J. Macintyre Henry. **R. W. Forsyth Ltd.,** Princes Street, Edinburgh (1907). Sir John Burnet, Tait and Lorne. **The Usher Hall,** Edinburgh (1914). J. Stockdale Harrison (of Leicester).

Transitional period (c. 1920–c. 1939)
Chemistry Building, University of Edinburgh, King's Buildings (1919–24). A. F. Balfour Paul (partner of Sir R. Rowand Anderson). **Department of Zoology,** University of Edinburgh, King's Buildings (1928). Sir Robert Lorimer. **City Chambers,** Glasgow (extension 1923). John Watson. **Scottish National War Memorial,** Edinburgh Castle (1928). Sir Robert Lorimer. **Scottish Legal Building,** Glasgow (1927). Wylie, Wright and Wylie. **200 St. Vincent Street,** Glasgow (1929). Burnet, Son and Dick. **St. John's Renfield Church,** Glasgow (1931). James Taylor Thomson. **Cosmo Cinema,** Glasgow (1939). W. J. Anderson (Junior). **St. Andrews House,** Edinburgh (1939). Thomas S. Tait of Sir J. Burnet, Tait and Lorne. **National Library of Scotland,** Edinburgh (1936–56). Dr. Reginald Fairlie. **Binns Ltd.,** Princes Street, Edinburgh (1936). J. R. McKay. **St. Andrew's (Episcopal) Cathedral,** Aberdeen (chancel extension and chapel—1941). Sir John Ninian Comper. **Portobello Power Station,** Edinburgh (1923). City Architect, Edinburgh.

Modern (c. 1945–70) Public and commercial buildings
Hydro-electric scheme, Glen Shira, Argyll (1955). Babtie, Shaw and Morton, engineers; Robert Hurd, architect. **Cockenzie Power Station,** East Lothian (1968). Kennedy and Donkin, engineers; Sir Robert Matthew, Johnson-Marshall and Partners, architects. **Killoch Colliery,** Ochiltry, Ayrshire (1958). Eigon Riss, architect. **Police Station,** Mayfield Road, Edinburgh (1963). Morris and Steedman. **County Offices,** Newton St. Boswells, Roxburghshire (1968). Peter Womersley. **Turnhouse Airport,** Edinburgh (1956, extended 1962). Sir Robert Matthew, Johnson-Marshall and Partners. **Plant House,** Royal Botanic Garden, Edinburgh (1967). G. A. Pearce, M.O.P.B. & W. **Forth Road Bridge** (1964). Mott, Hay and Anderson, engineers. **Standard Life Assurance Co.,** George Street, Edinburgh (extension) (1968). Michael Laird in association with Sir Robert Matthew. **British Home Stores,** Princes Street, Edinburgh (1968). Sir Robert Matthew, Johnson-Marshall and Partners.

Churches and hospitals
Kildrum Church, Cumbernauld (1963). Alan Reiach, Eric Hall and Partners. **St. Charles' R.C. Church,** Kelvinside Gardens, Glasgow (1960). Gillespie, Kidd and Coia. **St. John's Church,** Oxgangs, Edinburgh (1958). Alan Reiach and Partners. **The Nuffield Transplantation Surgery Unit,** Western General Hospital, Edinburgh (1968). Peter Womersley. **The Princess Margaret Rose Orthopaedic Hospital,** Edinburgh, (extension) (1961). Morris and Steedman.

Schools and university buildings
St. Crispin's School for Handicapped Children, Edinburgh (1964). Law and Dunbar-Nasmith. **Hutchesons' Boys' Grammar School,** Glasgow (1960). Boswell, Mitchell and Johnston. **King's Park Secondary School,** Glasgow (1964). Gillespie, Kidd and Coia. **Music School at George Watson's College,** Edinburgh (1964). Michael Laird. **David Hume Tower,** University of Edinburgh, George Square (1963). Sir Robert Matthew, Johnson-Marshall and Partners. **Animal Breeding Research Organisation Headquarters Building,** University of Edinburgh, King's Buildings (1964). Sir Basil Spence, Glover and Ferguson, Edinburgh. **Library,** University of Edinburgh, George Square (1967). Sir Basil Spence, Glover and Ferguson, Edinburgh. **Department of Pure and Applied Chemistry,** University of Strathclyde, Glasgow (1963). Walter Underwood and Partners.

Redevelopment and new towns
Dunbar Harbour Housing Development, East Lothian (1950). Sir Basil Spence. **Flats at Crathie Drive,** Partick, Glasgow (1952). Glasgow Corporation. **Cumbernauld New Town Development,** Dumbartonshire (designated 1956). **Leith Fort Housing Development,** Edinburgh (1963/64). Shaw Stewart and Perry.

Restoration and preservation schemes
St. Giles area, Pittenweem, Fife; Wheeler and Spronson. **Chessel's Court,** Canongate, Edinburgh; Robert Hurd and Partners. **Harbour area,** Portsoy, Banffshire; John J. Meldrum. **Inveraray,** Argyll; Ian G. Lindsay and Partners. **The Towers,** Dysart, Fife; Wheeler and Spronson.

Midlothian County Building, Edinburgh (1904). J. Macintyre Henry. A Neo-Classical design recalling a Renaissance palace.

Further reading

MACLEOD, ROBERT *Charles Rennie Mackintosh*
London, Country Life 1968
RICHARDS, J. M. *An Introduction to Modern Architecture*
London, Cassell 1961

GUIDES
EDINBURGH ARCHITECTURAL ASSOCIATION *Edinburgh—An Architectural Guide* Edinburgh 1964
YOUNG, A. McLAREN and DOAK, A. M. *Glasgow at a Glance* Glasgow, Collins 1965

PERIODICALS
The Architectural Review London, The Architectural Press (Monthly).
Concrete Quarterly London, Cement and Concrete Association.

Academic revivals and Art Nouveau 1900–c. 1914

Architectural design continued in the academic revival of the historical styles inherited from the Victorian era. Various forms of Neo-Classical design, exhibiting at times an almost Baroque (Late Renaissance) exuberance, were favoured for public and commercial buildings. In ecclesiastical architecture on the other hand Neo-Gothic and Romanesque were considered more appropriate. A renewed interest in the Scottish Vernacular, already evident at the end of the last century, made its appearance in the larger private house, villa and tenement.

The Art Nouveau style continued for the first decade and in Glasgow and its environs there are some notable examples. Early experiments with reinforced concrete and steel frame structures were bringing about a change in architectural design (see page 124).

The Usher Hall, Edinburgh (1914). J. Stockdale Harrison of Leicester. A Neo-Classical design, the winning design for a hall of 'simple and dignified appearance'.

McGeoch's, 28 West Campbell Street, Glasgow (1905).
Sir J. J. Burnet. An impressive building which makes a
feature of the vertical integration of the windows. This
was to become more common during the inter-war years.

Lion Chambers, Glasgow (1905). James Salmon II and
J. Gaff Gillespie. An early example in Scotland of the use
of reinforced concrete in a very tall building and a design
which shows a departure from the prevailing fashion.

Transitional period

Though signs of a change appeared before the First World War, the 'twenties and 'thirties were a transitional period for architecture in Scotland when most buildings showed the beginning of a real break with the past. Of those which displayed a past style, many now fairly obviously acknowledged steel frame construction and reinforced concrete and the advantages which these allow (e.g. larger window areas when the occasion demanded). On the whole, buildings tended to be plainer and more massive and showed some acknowledgement to the past in their proportions and detail.

In large buildings the vertical integration of the fenestration was usual and was one of the outward signs of the use of modern materials.

The design of municipal housing, though providing families with vastly better conditions, tended to be rather dull in appearance and monotonous in layout. In the field of private housing things were little better, the picturesque cottagey look was most popular. This originated from the new English domestic architecture and the Art Nouveau Movement but degenerated through tasteless mass production.

Scottish Legal Building, 95 Bothwell Street, Glasgow (1927). Wylie, Wright and Wylie.

St. Andrew's House, Edinburgh (1939). Thomas S. Tait of Sir John Burnet, Tait and Lorne.

Department of Zoology, University of Edinburgh (1928). Sir Robert Lorimer. A restrained Neo-Classical design, incorporating the advantages of modern steel windows. The construction is of steel and concrete with a cladding of sandstone.

National Library of Scotland, Edinburgh (1936–56). Dr. Reginald Fairlie. A design of massive Neo-Classical proportions, relieved by shallow decoration. An impressive and fairly typical design of the inter-war years. The structure consists of a framework of steel girders encased in concrete, with walls faced with dressed stone, and brick rendered with cement.

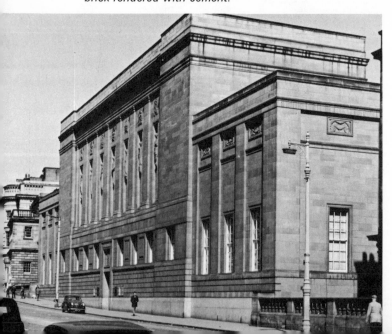

Modern c. 1945 — 70

Modern architectural design has developed as a natural consequence of the acceptance of machine production and the expanding science of building. Therefore when we look at the new architecture going up around us we can appreciate it only if we remind ourselves of this. The modern idiom can be interpreted with as much success in vast engineering structures as in any other type of building, and in this respect differs from earlier architecture.

Popular means of communication (press, T.V., radio and exhibitions) have done a lot to familiarise us with the architecture of today. Much can be learnt by watching the construction of new buildings. On most large-scale developments, display signs give the names of the architect and the various specialised contractors who are involved on the site. When important public buildings and areas of redevelopment are announced in the press, these are often followed by exhibitions of drawings and scale models. This gives us an opportunity to become familiar with the proposed work, and helps us to judge its artistic merit when it is completed.

Nuffield Transplantation Surgery Unit, Western General Hospital, Edinburgh (1968). Peter Womersley.

Modern and traditional materials

The Hennébique system of reinforced concrete was invented late in the 19th century in France. Its peculiar structural qualities were quickly appreciated and it was soon widely used. But because of the strong academic tradition its effect upon design in the early years was not often seen (see page 124). During the inter-war years it was an important contributory factor in the changed appearance of buildings (see page 126). Subsequently, together with other new developments it has been responsible for a completely new conception of architectural design (see above).

The diagrams illustrate simply the principle of reinforced concrete. When a steel bar is incorporated in concrete in the area of tension it will sustain a heavy load. The method of its construction makes it possible to design structures for different kinds of loading and into any desired shape. Besides allowing for greater flexibility in design it makes possible for instance the enclosure of larger areas, wider openings and thinner walls.

The Nuffield Surgery Unit is a reinforced concrete

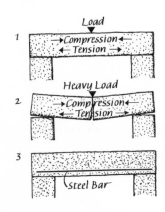

structure designed for a specific medical purpose. In meeting its special requirements, e.g. filtered ventilation and windows guarded against the direct rays of the sun, the designer has created a building of impressive architectural merit.

The term 'fair face' is used when a building material is left without an applied surface finish. In the interesting

example on the left, the steel girders supporting roof and floors of concrete slabs are free standing outside the building. This both meets fire regulations and gives more room within. The walls are merely screens. Traditional materials—brick and timber—have been incorporated in the facing.

The Plant House is a light and graceful metal and glass construction taking advantage of an undulating site. The main steel supporting arches are on the *outside* suspended from wires; this prevents corrosion from humidity. The use of non-ferrous metal for the glazing bars reduces the need for maintenance and interference with the plants. The beauty of this building is in the lightness and spaciousness of its structure, so providing natural conditions for the development of plants and unobstructed viewing by the visitor.

Animal Breeding Research Organisation Headquarters Building, King's Buildings, University of Edinburgh (1964). Sir Basil Spence, Glover and Ferguson, Edinburgh.

The New Plant House, Royal Botanic Garden, Edinburgh (1967). G. A. Pearce, Ministry of Public Building and Works.

Traditional building materials are used extensively in combination with modern materials and methods in architectural design today. Their excellent weathering properties and pleasing appearance have made them much sought after. This, together with a fresh appreciation of vernacular architecture has resulted in many pleasing designs of a more national character, particularly noticeable in the domestic field, clubs and churches.

School, Fintry, Stirlingshire (1968). Weir Housing Corporation Ltd. A combination of timber and natural stone.

Housing redevelopment and restoration, Dysart, Fife (1965). Wheeler & Spronson. Colour-washed harling and timber provide a traditional finish for the modern houses shown on the left of the picture. On the right is The Towers, a 16th century building which has been given a new lease of life by skilful restoration.

Kildrum Church, Cumbernauld, Dumbartonshire (1963). Alan Reiach, Eric W. Hall and Partners. Good modern design has been carried out in traditional materials— brick and wood—in this attractive church interior.

New Music School at George Watson's College, Edinburgh (1964). Michael Laird. The unusual form of this building was the outcome of a careful study of its requirements. The ventilation recesses provided at each practice room, and the hyperbolic parabolic roof (of light timber construction), which makes a column-free auditorium, are interesting features.

Distillery warehouses, Muirhall, Edinburgh (1966). Blyth & Blyth, engineers; Michael Laird, architect. The steel-framed warehouse buildings have walls built of dark blue brick and aluminium sheet is used for roof covering.

Housing development, Dunbar Harbour, East Lothian (1950). Sir Basil Spence, Glover and Ferguson, Edinburgh. New houses which reflect traditional design.

A private house, near Turnberry, Ayrshire (1963). Peter Womersley. In his design the architect has attractively related this house to its natural setting and at the same time let its owners derive most enjoyment from its exposed position. The house is basically timber-framed construction, sitting on a stone base.

Interior of private house at Turnberry. Peter Womersley. The elegant simplicity and spaciousness of this 'open-plan' interior are in accord with the natural setting of the house.

British Home Stores, Edinburgh (1968). Sir Robert Matthew, Johnson-Marshall and Partners.

Standard Life Assurance Co., Edinburgh (extension 1968). Michael Laird in consultation with Sir Robert Matthew.

Two buildings in Georgian Edinburgh which respect their architectural settings, without being in any way imitative, are an office extension and a department store (British Home Stores).

St. Charles' R.C. Church, Kelvinside Gardens, Glasgow (1960). Gillespie, Kidd and Coia.

Private House, Edinburgh (1961). Morris and Steedman.

New housing at Cable's Wynd, Leith (1965). Alison and
Hutchison and Partners.

Princess Margaret Rose Orthopaedic Hospital, Edinburgh,
extension (1961). Morris and Steedman.

Industrialised systems

Fully industrialised systems of building, involving the use of factory-made components throughout—walls, floors, windows, doors, sanitation, etc—are as yet carried out only on a limited scale. (An early example of this was the post-war 'pre-fab'.) Though this method of building is technically advanced there is only a small demand for manufacturers to go into production. When there is wider agreement amongst clients, i.e. local authorities and private concerns, about standardisation of components, this may well become the most widely used building method. It is interesting to reflect that a kind of standardisation existed already as a unifying element in Georgian architecture.

A body concerned with promoting improved techniques in industrialised and traditional aspects of building is the National Building Agency. The N.B.A. provides an advisory service for architects, builders and local authorities, and is sometimes commissioned to prepare designs, as in the special circumstances of the Highland School Hostels.

The hostels are designed on an industrialised system to fulfil a very special need, where the remoteness of their situation, scarcity of labour and great urgency were important factors. A 'kit' of standard parts was designed which allowed for assembly in various ways to meet the need of hostels of different sizes and varying site conditions. This system resulted in a saving of cost and time.

Dunoon Grammar School Hostel for Argyll County Council (1968). The National Building Agency Scottish Office.

High-rise development, Paisley, in which industrialised techniques have been employed. Such multi-storeyed housing is built to overcome the problems of overcrowding and scarcity of land. The standardised wall panels, some with, some without windows, are arranged to suit the internal requirements.

Shopping centre and housing redevelopment, Cambus-lang, Lanarkshire (1965). Samuel McCall, County Architect.

Heddell's Park, Lerwick, Shetland (1959). Moira and Moira.

New towns and redevelopment

The earliest town planning in Scotland dates from the 18th century. The layouts were conceived as appropriate settings for the architecture of the time.

Since the last war Town and Country Planning Acts have placed the responsibility for redevelopment in the hands of local authorities. Architects and town planners collaborate, designing for whole communities, taking into account the varied needs of the present day. Spacious traffic-free shopping precincts, service roads and play areas, etc. feature normally in their layouts, contrasting with the monotonous sprawl of pre-war housing schemes.

Cumbernauld, Dumbartonshire, designated a New Town in 1956.

Split-level houses at Cumbernauld New Town (Seafar). These houses built on a slope, are entered at intermediate level so that one goes upstairs to the living room and dining-kitchen and downstairs to two bedrooms and bathroom. The area has been attractively landscaped with trees and shrubs, and this, added to the intimacy of the layout, is conducive to pleasant living conditions.

Cumbernauld New Town is an outstanding example of community architecture. The buildings are grouped to form neighbourhoods in a variety of lay-outs, safely away from the main roads which are thus left unimpeded.

Upper Shira Dam, near Inveraray, Argyll, built for the North of Scotland Hydro-Electric Board (1955). Babtie, Shaw and Morton, civil engineers; Robert Hurd, architect.

Industrial architecture and structural engineering

Hydro-electric schemes have shown a consistently high standard of architectural and engineering design since their inception.

Upper Shira Dam is a good example of this post-war work. It is 714 metres long and constructed mainly of mass concrete. It forms part of the system feeding the Clachan hydro-electric power station in the Glen Shira Scheme.

Killoch Colliery, Ochiltry, Ayrshire (1958). Built for the National Coal Board. Egon Riss, architect. Two winder towers at the pithead.

Forth Road Bridge (1964). Mott, Hay and Anderson, engineers.

The heavy demands of road traffic are being met with carefully designed systems of roads and served by bridges which at their best are light and graceful in appearance.

Ness Bridge, Inverness (1961). Sir Murdoch MacDonald, engineer.

General reading

The following publications give information about places open to the public:

Guides to individual ancient monuments and historic buildings in the care of the Ministry of Public Building and Works, H.M.S.O.

BARTHOLOMEW AND SON LTD. [Steer, K. A., Editor] *Historic Buildings open to the public* and principal antiquities older than A.D. 1100, a map of South East Scotland, Edinburgh 1961

CHILDE, V. GORDON and SIMPSON, W. DOUGLAS *Illustrated Guide to Ancient Monuments* (Vol. VI *Scotland*) Edinburgh, H.M.S.O. 5th edition 1967

FLEMING, JOHN *Scottish Country Houses and Gardens open to the public* London, Country Life 1954

INDEX PUBLICATIONS *Historic Houses, Castles and Gardens in Great Britain and Ireland* London (Annually)

THE NATIONAL TRUST FOR SCOTLAND *Year Book* Edinburgh

THE NATIONAL TRUST FOR SCOTLAND IN ASSOCIATION WITH THE COUNTRYSIDE COMMISSION FOR SCOTLAND AND THE SCOTTISH TOURIST BOARD *Seeing Scotland* Edinburgh

Books about particular areas

A detailed account is contained in the county *Inventories* of the Royal Commission on the Ancient and Historical Monuments of Scotland, H.M.S.O., of which the following have been published: Berwickshire; Caithness; Dumfriesshire; East Lothian; City of Edinburgh; Fife, Kinross and Clackmannan; Kirkcudbrightshire; Midlothian and West Lothian; Outer Hebrides, Skye and the Small Isles; Orkney; Peeblesshire; Roxburghshire; Selkirkshire; Shetland; Stirlingshire; Sutherland; Wigtownshire.

In addition the following provide information about the local scene:

Dundee:

WALKER, D. M. *Architects and Architecture in Dundee 1770–1914* Abertay Historical Society 1955

Edinburgh:

CROSSLAND, J. BRIAN *Victorian Edinburgh* Letchworth Wayfair 1966

EDINBURGH ARCHITECTURAL ASSOCIATION *Edinburgh—An Architectural Guide* Edinburgh 1964

LINDSAY, IAN G. *Old Edinburgh* Edinburgh, Oliver and Boyd 1947

LINDSAY, IAN G. *Georgian Edinburgh* Edinburgh, Oliver and Boyd 1948

YOUNGSON, A. J. *The Making of Classical Edinburgh, 1750–1840* Edinburgh, University Press 1966

Fife:

CENTRAL AND NORTH FIFE PRESERVATION SOCIETY [Cant, Ronald G.] *Central and North Fife, an Illustrated Survey of its Landscape and Architecture* Cupar 1965

ST. ANDREWS PRESERVATION TRUST [Cant, Ronald G.] *Old St. Andrews* 1947

Glasgow:

CANT, RONALD G. and LINDSAY, IAN G. *Old Glasgow* Edinburgh, Oliver and Boyd 1947

GOMME, ANDOR and WALKER, DAVID *Architecture of Glasgow* London, Lund Humphries 1968

YOUNG, ANDREW McLAREN and DOAK, A. M. *Glasgow at a Glance* Glasgow, Collins 1965

Moray:

ELGIN SOCIETY [Cant, Ronald G. and Lindsay, Ian G.] *Old Moray* Elgin 1948

ELGIN SOCIETY [Cant, Ronald G. and Lindsay, Ian G.] *Old Elgin* Elgin 1954

Stirling:

CANT, RONALD G. and LINDSAY, IAN G. *Old Stirling* Edinburgh, Oliver and Boyd 1948

Architecture: general

DUNBAR, JOHN G. *The Historic Architecture of Scotland* London, Batsford 1966

HANNAH, IAN C. *Story of Scotland in Stone* Edinburgh, Oliver and Boyd 1934

HITCHCOCK, HENRY-RUSSELL *Early Victorian Architecture in Britain* 2 vols., London, Architectural Press and New Haven University Press, Yale 1954

MAXWELL, SIR JOHN STIRLING *Shrines and Homes of Scotland* London, Maclehose 1937 (Reprinted by Chambers 1958)

RICHARDS, J. M. *An Introduction to Modern Architecture* London, Cassell 1961 (Revised) (Originally published by Penguin Books 1940)

SCOTT-MONCRIEFF, GEORGE (Editor) *The Stones of Scotland* London, Batsford 1938

SIMPSON, W. DOUGLAS *The Ancient Stones of Scotland* London, Hale 1965

SUMMERSON, JOHN *The Architecture in Britain, 1530–1830* London, Penguin Books 1953 (4th Edition 1965)

Castle and house

BARLEY, M. W. *The House and Home: A Visual History of Modern Britain* London, Vista Books 1963

CRUDEN, STEWART *The Scottish Castle* Edinburgh, Nelson 1963 (Revised)

HILL, OLIVER *Scottish Castles of the 16th and 17th Centuries* London, Country Life 1953

MACGIBBON, D. and ROSS, T. *The Castellated and Domestic Architecture of Scotland* 5 vols. Edinburgh, David Douglas 1887—92

MACKENZIE, W. MACKAY *The Mediaeval Castle in Scotland* London, Methuen 1927

SIMPSON, W. DOUGLAS *Scottish Castles* Edinburgh, H.M.S.O. 1964 (4th Impression)

SINCLAIR, COLIN *The Thatched Houses of the Old Highlands* Edinburgh, Oliver and Boyd 1953

TRANTER, NIGEL G. *The Fortified House in Scotland* 4 vols. Edinburgh, Oliver and Boyd 1962—

Church

CRUDEN, STEWART *Scottish Abbeys* Edinburgh, H.M.S.O. 1960

HAY, GEORGE *The Architecture of Scottish Post-Reformation Churches, 1560—1843* Oxford, Clarendon Press 1957

LINDSAY, IAN G. *The Scottish Parish Kirk* Edinburgh, St. Andrews Press 1960

MACGIBBON, D. and ROSS, T. *The Ecclesiastical Architecture of Scotland* 3 vols. Edinburgh, David Douglas 1896—97

Industry

BUTT, JOHN *Industrial Archaeology of Scotland* Newton Abbot, David and Charles 1967

BUTT, JOHN; DONNACHIE, IAN L; HUME, JOHN R. *Industrial History in Pictures—Scotland* Newton Abbot, David and Charles 1968

Decoration

APTED, M. R. *The Painted Ceilings of Scotland, 1550—1650* Edinburgh, H.M.S.O. 1966

CRUDEN, STEWART *The Early Christian and Pictish Monuments of Scotland* Edinburgh, H.M.S.O. 1964 (2nd Edition)

RICHARDSON, JAMES S. *The Mediaeval Stone Carver in Scotland* Edinburgh, University Press 1964

Biographies

FLEMING, JOHN *Robert Adam and His Circle* London, Murray 1962

MACLEOD, ROBERT *Charles Rennie Mackintosh* London, Hamlyn for Country Life 1968

ROLT, L. T. C. *Thomas Telford* London, Longmans 1958 (4th Impression 1965)

Reference

FLEMING, JOHN; HONOUR, HUGH; PEVSNER, NIKOLAUS *The Penguin Dictionary of Architecture* Harmondsworth, Penguin Books 1966

PEHNT, WOLFGANG (Editor) *Encyclopedia of Modern Architecture* London, Thames and Hudson 1963

Prehistory

FEACHEM, RICHARD *A Guide to Prehistoric Scotland* London, Batsford 1963

PIGGOTT, STUART *Scotland Before History* Edinburgh, Nelson 1958

RIVET, A. L. F. (Editor) *The Iron Age in Northern Britain* Edinburgh, University Press 1966

SCOTT, JACK G. *Regional Archaeologies—South West Scotland* London, Heineman 1966

History

DICKINSON, WILLIAM CROFT *Scotland from the Earliest Times to 1603. A New History of Scotland* Vol. 1 Edinburgh, Nelson 1961 (2nd revised edition 1965)

PRYDE, GEORGE S. *Scotland from 1603 to the present day. A New History of Scotland* Vol. II Edinburgh, Nelson 1962

Periodicals which will help the reader to keep abreast with modern developments in Britain:
The Architectural Review London, The Architectural Press (Monthly)
Concrete Quarterly London, Cement and Concrete Association

Time chart showing the approximate relationship between historical background and the main building periods with examples. The examples are not necessarily of one period as their construction was often protracted. It must be remembered too, that the periods overlap creating transitional phases.

Time Chart

	Historical background	Periods	Building examples — Religious	Others
3000		Neolithic Age		
2000		Bronze Age	Maeshowe, Orkney	Skara Brae, Orkney
			Callanish Standing Stones, Lewis	
1000				
B.C.		Iron Age		Broch, Mousa, Shetland
A.D.	Roman Invasions	Roman		Forts—Antonine Wall
	St. Columba		Brough of Deerness, Orkney	Beehive-cells, Garvelloch Isles
1000	Norsemen	EARLY CHRISTIAN—CELTIC	Round Tower, Brechin, Angus	Norse Longhouse, Jarlshof, Shetland
	Duncan I		St. Peter's Church, Birsay, Orkney	
	Malcolm III m. Margaret		'Margaret's' Church, Dunfermline Abbey	
1100	David I	NORMAN—ROMANESQUE	Dunfermline Abbey, Fife	Duffus Castle Morayshire
			Dalmeny Church, W. Lothian	
			Jedburgh Abbey, Roxburghshire	
1200		EARLY GOTHIC	Glasgow Cathedral	Mingary Castle, Argyll
			Dunstaffnage Chapel, Argyll	Dirleton Castle, E. Lothian
1300	Wars of Independence			Kildrummy Castle, Aberdeenshire
			Sweetheart Abbey, Kirkcudbrightshire	Drum Castle, Aberdeenshire
		MIDDLE GOTHIC		Tantallon Castle, E. Lothian
1400			Melrose Abbey, Roxburghshire	Doune Castle, Perthshire
				Borthwick Castle, Midlothian
				Palace, Linlithgow, W. Lothian
			St. Michael's Church, Linlithgow,	
1500		LATE GOTHIC	Seton Collegiate Church, E. Lothian	Affleck Castle, Angus
			King's College, Aberdeen	Palace, Stirling
	Reformation			Claypotts Castle, Angus
			Chapel Royal, Stirling	Town of Culross, Fife
1600	Union of the Crowns			Craigievar Castle, Aberdeenshire
		EARLY SCOTS RENAISSANCE	Lyne Church, Peeblesshire	George Heriot's Hospital, Edinburgh
			Canongate Church, Edinburgh	Palace of Holyrood, Edinburgh
1700	Union of Parliaments	GEORGIAN—CLASSICAL		Duff House, Banff
			Auldearn Church, Nairnshire	Hopetoun House, W. Lothian
			St. Andrew's Church, Glasgow	Edinburgh New Town
1800		LATE GEORGIAN Neo Gothic Neo Classical	Ceres Church, Fife	Culzean Castle, Ayrshire
			St. John's Church, Edinburgh	Dunninald Castle, Angus
		VICTORIAN	Lansdowne Church, Glasgow	Old Royal High School, Edinburgh
				Donaldson's Hospital, Edinburgh
				Forth Bridge
1900	First World War		National War Memorial, Edinburgh	Glasgow School of Art
		MODERN		National Library, Edinburgh
			St. Charles' Church, Glasgow	Glen Shira Dams, Argyll
				Cumbernauld New Town

Growth of a National Style

143

Glossary

abacus   a slab forming the top of a capital

aisle   the lengthwise divisions of a church parallel to the nave and chancel

apse   a semi-circular or multiangular termination to a chamber

arcade   a series of arched openings resting on columns or piers

ashlar   dressed and squared building stone

aumbry   a recess in a wall used as a cupboard

barbican   the forward extension of a castle entrance

barmkin   a defensive wall around a castle or tower house

barrel vault   an arched roof of round or pointed section

boss   a raised ornament at the junction of the ribs of a Gothic vault

broach spire   an octagonal spire rising from an inter-penetrating pyramid

buttress   a projecting support against a wall to counter the thrust of an arch or vault

capital   the crowning member of a column

chancel   the eastern part of a church reserved for the clergy and choir

chapter house   place of assembly in a monastery where the daily affairs of the Order were attended to

chase   a groove or channel

choir or **quire**   part of a church between the nave and presbytery for the choir

clearstory or **clerestory**   a row of windows in the upper wall of a chamber above adjoining roof levels

cloister   a covered arcade surrounding a courtyard or garden in a monastery

colonnade   a series of columns

corbel   a projection from a wall to support timbers or masonry

crenellation   square indentations at intervals along a parapet

crow-stepped   stepped stones of a gable

cushion capital   a capital of cushion-like form

cusp   the point made between foils in Gothic tracery

donjon   the strongest tower in a medieval castle, sometimes called the keep

dormer window   a window with its own gable rising from a wall head

dorter   a monastic dormitory

dry-stone   stone laid without mortar

embrasure   a splayed opening for an arrow-slit or window

finial   an ornamental top to a gable, pinnacle or spire

foil   a small arc in Gothic tracery

frater   a monastic dining hall

garth   a cloistered courtyard or garden

hammer-beam roof   a gabled roof supported on timber brackets without tie-beams

harling   a rendering for external walls made of lime and small stones

hourding or **hoarding**   a projecting timber gallery at the wall head of a medieval castle

jamb   the internal side of a door or window

keep   see donjon

lean-to   a sloping roof projecting from a wall

lintel   a beam over an opening

machicolation   spaces between corbels allowing a downward view of the wall face

nave   the western part of a church as opposed to the chancel

newel   the central shaft of a circular stair

niche   a recess in a wall or buttress commonly for a statue

parapet   a low wall

pediment   the triangular termination of the roof of a Classical building

pend   a vaulted passage-way

pier   a mass of supporting masonry between the openings of a wall; also the supports of a bridge

pilaster   a shallow rectangular projection on a wall resembling a column

pinnacle   a vertical structure resembling a small turret

plinth   the lowest member of a column; also the splayed base of a building

portcullis   a grating which can be lowered to close an entrance

postern   a small side entrance to a castle, a sally port

presbytery   part of a church at the eastern end reserved for the priest

quire   see choir

rampart   a defensive bank around a fortification

range   a line of connected buildings

rood screen   a screen surmounted by a crucifix separating the chancel from the nave

sacristy   a place in a church where the sacred vessels are kept

sanctuary   the most sacred part of a church at the eastern end

screens   a partition across the lower end of a medieval hall

skew-put   the corner stone of a gable

solar   a private apartment

strap-work   flat interlaced pattern-work

string course   a horizontal projecting moulding on the face of a building

144

tie-beam   a horizontal beam securing the lower ends of rafters

tirling pin   a device on a door-latch for rattling

tracery   Gothic ornamental openwork as in the upper part of windows

transept   the arms of a cruciform church at right angles to the nave

triforium   a gallery between the clearstory and the nave arcade

tympanum   the recessed face of a pediment; also the space between the lintel and arch of a doorway

undercroft   a vaulted basement or crypt beneath a main chamber

vault   an arched ceiling

wynd   a narrow passage-way between buildings

yett   a hinged iron grating at the entrance to a castle or tower-house

Index to Places

Fendoch 8
Ferniehirst 58
Fettercairn 88
Fiddes 58
Finavon 2
Fintry 129
Fochabers 91 101
Fordell 70
Forth Bridges 107 116 121 140 143
Fortrose 38
Fowlis Easter 46
Fyvie 70

Garvelloch Isles 10 143
Gifford 90–1
Glamis 70 79
Glasgow 25 27 33–5 38 46 57 64 69 89 90–1 101–3 106–7 111–14 118–21 124–5 134 143
Glen Elg 2
Glen Shira 121 139 143
Glenbuchart 58
Glenorchy 107
Grandtully 58
Grangemouth 89
Grantown-on-Spey 91 101
Greenknowe 58

Haddington 46 70 91
Haddo 90
Hailes 26 58
Hallbar 58
Hallforest 37
Hawick 15
Hayhope Knowe 2
Hermitage 45
Hill House 120
Hopetoun 70 80 92–4 96 143
Huntingtower 45 50 58 61–3 70
Huntly 15 45 58 70
Hutton 107

Inchcolm 27
Inchtuthill 8
Innes 70
Inveraray 90–1 95 97 101 104 121 139
Inverarity 91
Inverkeithing 70
Inverlochy 26 29 69
Inverness 69 140
Invernochty 15 19
Inverurie 15 17
Iona 10

Jedburgh 16 26 143

Kelso 16 22 107
Kemback 58
Kilbarchan 98
Kildrummy 26 29 30 40 52 143
Killean 27
Kilmartin 58
Kilmory 27 36
Kilpeck (Herefordshire) 24
Kincardine-in-Menteith 107
Kincardine o'Neil 27

Kinclaven 26
Kinross 70 74
Kintore 91
Kirkcaldy 90
Kirkcudbright 58 70
Kirkliston 16
Kirkmadrine 10
Kirkton 46 53

Lanark, New 105 107 117
    Old 90
Larkhall 119
Lauder 70
Leith Hall 70
Leslie 70
Letham 89
Lethendy 70
Leuchars 16 25
Lewis, Island of 2 4 14 143
Lincluden 38 46
Linhouse 58
Linlithgow 46 50–2 54–5 57 72 87 143
Linton 16 24
Loanhead 2
Loch Doon 26
Lochhouse 58
Lochindorb 26
Lochleven 37
Luffness 58
Lumphanan 15 16 19
Lyne 8 70 80 143

Mearns 45
Melgund 58
Mellerstain 90
Melrose 38 43–4 46 54 106 143
Melville Castle 90
Melville House 70 90
Midmar 58
Mingary 26 28 143
Moffat House 90
Montrose 90 106
Morton 26
Muchalls 58
Muthill 16

Neidpath 37
Nether Largie 2
Newark 45 58
Newcastleton 90–1 101
Newlands 106
Newstead 8
Newton St. Boswells 121

Ochiltry 121 139
Orchardton 45
Orkneys 1–6 10 11 13 15 16 26 58 70 74 143
Overtoun 114

Paisley 27 46 136
Pencaitland 27
Penicuik 91
Perth 46 57 69 88–9 106
Pitfour 90
Pittenweem 121
Pluscarden 21 27

Portsoy 121
Preston Hall 90
Prestongrange 58
Prestonpans 27 45 70 85–6 88

Rahoy 2
Rait 26 32
Ravenscraig 45–6
Reay 91
Repentance 70
Restenneth 10
Rosslyn 46
Rosyth 58
Rothesay 16 19 26

St. Andrews 16 21 57 69 70 82–3 121
St. Bean's 58
St. Kentigern's 27
St. Monance 38
Sanquhar 91
Sauchie 45
Scone 106
Scotstarvet 70
Seton 46 53–4 143
Shetlands 1 2 4 6 7 10 13 26 58 70 137 143
Skelmorlie 81
Skipness 26
Smailholm 58
Spedlin's Tower 70
Stirling 46 57–9 67 70–1 85 91 106 143
Stobo 16
Sweetheart 21 38 42 143

Tantallon 37 40 143
Terpersie 58
Threave 37
Tioram 26–7
Tobermory 91
Tolquhon 58
Tomintoul 91
Torphichen 46
Torthorwald 37
Torwoodhead 58
Towie Barclay 58
Traprain Law 2
Traquair 58 62 64
Tulliallan 26 70
Tulliebardine 46
Turnberry 132
Tynninghame 16

Ullapool 91
Urquhart 2 15
Urr, Mote of 15

Walston 70
Weem 58
West Plean 4
West Wemyss 91
White Hill 2
Whithorn 10
Windyhill 120
Winton 70

Yester 26 90